THE CONSTITUTIONAL MONARCHY IN FRANCE, 1814–48

The Constitutional Monarchy in France, 1814–48

PAMELA PILBEAM

 LONGMAN

An imprint of **PEARSON EDUCATION**

Harlow, England · London · New York · Reading · Massachusetts · San Francisco ·
Toronto · Don Mills, Ontario · Sydney · Tokyo · Singapore · Hong Kong · Seoul ·
Taipei · Cape Town · Madrid · Mexico City · Amsterdam · Munich · Paris · Milan

Pearson Education Limited
Edinburgh Gate
Harlow
Essex CM20 2JE
England

and Associated Companies throughout the world

Visit us on the world wide web at:
www.pearsoned-ema.com

First published 2000

ISBN 0 582 31210 8 PPR

British Library Cataloguing-in-Publication Data
A catalogue record for this book is available from the British Library

Library of Congress Cataloging-in-Publication Data
A catalog record for this book is available from the Library of Congress

Set by 7 in 10/12 Sabon
Printed in Malaysia, KVP

CONTENTS

AN INTRODUCTION TO THE SERIES

Such is the pace of historical enquiry in the modern world that there is an ever-widening gap between the specialist article or monograph, incorporating the results of current research, and general surveys, which inevitably become out of date. *Seminar Studies in History* are designed to bridge this gap. The series was founded by Patrick Richardson in 1966 and his aim was to cover major themes in British, European and World history. Between 1980 and 1996 Roger Lockyer continued his work, before handing the editorship over to Clive Emsley and Gordon Martel. Clive Emsley is Professor of History at the Open University, while Gordon Martel is Professor of International History at the University of Northern British Columbia, Canada and Senior Research Fellow at De Montfort University.

All the books are written by experts in their field who are not only familiar with the latest research but have often contributed to it. They are frequently revised, in order to take account of new information and interpretations. They provide a selection of documents to illustrate major themes and provoke discussion, and also a guide to further reading. The aim of *Seminar Studies* is to clarify complex issues without over-simplifying them, and to stimulate readers into deepening their knowledge and understanding of major themes and topics.

NOTE ON REFERENCING SYSTEM

Readers should note that numbers in square brackets [5] refer them to the corresponding entry in the Bibliography at the end of the book (specific page numbers are given in italics). A number in square brackets preceded by *Doc.* [*Doc. 5*] refers readers to the corresponding item in the Documents section which follows the main text.

ACKNOWLEDGEMENTS

The publishers would like to thank the following for permission to reproduce copyright material: Dover Publications, New York for reproduction of photographs of the lithographs 'Rue Transnonain 15 April 1834', 'The Main Actor in a Tragi-comedy 29 March 1835' and 'A Journey Among Oppressed Peoples, 14 August 1834' by Daumier, published in *Daumier, 120 Great Lithographs* by Ramus in 1979.

Whilst every effort has been made to trace the owners of copyright material, in a few cases this has proved to be problematic and so we take this opportunity to offer our appologies to any copyright holders whose rights we may have unwittingly infringed.

PREFACE

Why did France experience so much political upheaval between 1814 and 1848? The First Restoration in 1814 was interrupted a year later by Napoleon's Hundred Day return. In 1830 Charles X was despatched from the throne by a revolution and in 1848 Louis-Philippe followed suit, in not dissimilar circumstances. During the 1830s there were repeated smaller revolts and riots. Yet the structure of the constitutional monarchy was barely altered by the 1830 revolution, nor was its ruling elite. Political insurrection was accompanied by considerable stability in state institutions.

A similar paradox was visible in the social framework. The motor of revolution was invariably popular insurrection, fomented by much-publicised class tension and socio-economic deprivation among artisans and peasants. Socialists projected new worlds of radical social change. Feminists urged that French law recognise women as equal adults. Yet France remained dominated by a wealthy, male elite throughout these years, part noble, part bourgeois, which owed its position to property, mainly land, and the control of official appointments. 1830 changed the names, not the fundamental principles of government. These were years of only modest population growth and of a gradual move to a market economy. Beneath anxious discourse over the 'social question' and fears of class war, there were no major shocks to the social structure. This volume will consider the relationship between the memory of, and repeated self-conscious 'action replays' of the 1789 revolution and the ubiquitous search for a 'middle way' in these years. What did the revolutions signify and why did the French not arrive at a settled form of government?

PART ONE: INTRODUCTION

1 RESTORATIONS 1814–15

THE FIRST RESTORATION, 1814

The Bourbon Monarchy has been condemned by recent historians as 'impossible'. How impossible [72; 169; 182]? The two Bourbon Restorations, the first in April 1814 and the second in July 1815, were not the product of popular monarchist movements in France, but solely the consequence of Napoleon's defeat by Allied troops [118]. There was nothing inevitable about the Quadruple Alliance, which was merely cobbled together by the 1813 Treaty of Chaumont. Collapse could have occurred at any stage, given the degree of mutual suspicion and rivalry among the Allies: Britain, Russia, Prussia and Austria. There was nothing inevitable about their victories, nor the subsequent destruction of the Empire. This is not to say that the Empire was universally popular, but by 1814 22 years of warfare was beginning to seem less than a patriotic adventure, particularly considering the costly defeats in Spain and Russia (1812). However the Imperial regiments showed staunch loyalty to Napoleon, even after the comprehensive defeats of 1814 and 1815.

There was no immediate, obvious alternative to Napoleon. The majority of politically active and ambitious individuals, including republicans and former monarchists, had been employed by the Empire and were unlikely to forego their income lightly. Napoleon had been careful to secure as much support from rival factions as he could. There was no alternative republican consensus. The Jacobin phase of the Republic had been equated with the Terror by the propagandists of the Directory, Consulate and Empire.

The decision to restore the Bourbon dynasty was made by the Allies on pragmatic grounds; alternatives were seriously debated, including the Orleanist branch of the family represented by Louis-Philippe, duc d'Orléans. However, Louis-Philippe remained loyal to his Bourbon cousins, with whom he had shared two decades of exile, unlike his father, who during the Revolution had called himself

Philippe-Egalité and, as a member of the Convention voted the death of his cousin, the king. The Allies also considered one of the many dispossessed German princes as well as Bernadotte, one of Napoleon's generals, whom Napoleon had made ruler of Sweden and who subsequently had rebelled against him. The Allies finally settled for Louis XVI's two brothers, the comte de Provence, old and childless, to be succeeded by his brother, the comte d'Artois; in the event they seemed the least disruptive, most malleable choice. Their resettlement had the additional benefit that it would also eliminate the huge cost of supporting the *émigrés*, which represented a substantial charge on Britain. The final structure of the new system of government owed something to British ideology too; as the chief paymaster of the Allied war effort and the only state with a limited monarchy, Britain insisted that Louis XVIII be restored in tandem with a constitutional parliamentary system similar to its own.

THE CONSTITUTIONAL CHARTER OF 1814

How similar? The Allied armies entered Paris on 31 March 1814. On 6 April the rump of Napoleon's Senate, called together by Talleyrand, Napoleon's Minister of Foreign Affairs and an adroit turn-coat, made the first independent decision of its life in offering a royal throne to the comte de Provence, if he would rule in conjunction with them. Louis XVIII promptly commissioned nine from the Senate, nine from Napoleon's equally powerless Legislative Body and three of his own appointees to write a constitution [98]. The Constitutional Charter of 4 June 1814 was a stitched-together compromise. This can be demonstrated by the fact that on the day of its publication Louis added a preamble, never discussed by the committee [*Doc. 1*].

This preamble exemplified the long-treasured aspirations of the *émigrés*. The constitution, a 'charter', was, it claimed, 'octroyée', given to the people by the grace and favour of a king in the twenty-first year of his reign, and in line with charters granted by his forefathers. The writer claimed that it was 'Divine providence' that had facilitated the king's return. Louis's title also assumed that his elder brother's son, who died in prison, had been king. The main part of the constitution sounded less divine and far more the result of human negotiation [*Doc. 2*]. Its clauses spelled out a compromise in which the king acquired an hereditary throne under certain conditions. Most important, he was to govern in combination with a parliament, of a kind that no revolutionary constitution had ever envisaged. This consisted of a Chamber of Deputies of 258 elected members and a Chamber of Peers, nominated by the king. The deputies were to be directly elected by all adult male taxpayers of 30 years and more who paid at least 500 francs in direct taxes. During the Restoration (1814–30) there were never more than 100,000 qualified voters out of a total population of around 32.5 millions. With a requirement that candidates pay an annual tax bill of 1,000 francs and be at least 40 years of age, the number of potential candidates was a mere 15,000. The king would nominate peers, either for life, or with hereditary tenure. At first the vast majority were former Napoleonic senators, but subsequent nominations favoured loyal royalists.

Parliament had the right to discuss and vote all legislation. All taxation had to be approved first by the deputies. Article 14 allowed the king to make decrees in an emergency without consulting the assembly. The king would select his own ministers. The constitution said they were 'responsible', but did not specify to whom. At first these ambiguities were not significant. Both kings were careful to choose ministers and propose legislation acceptable to the deputies. Clearly this was not a full-blown parliamentary system and neither assembly had a direct say in ministerial appointments, but it did provide France with a novel constitutional framework (11; 46; 72; 111).

THE INSTITUTIONS OF THE EMPIRE THAT SURVIVED IN THE MONARCHY

The constitutional arrangements of 1814 marked a positive attempt to invent a workable combination of royal and parliamentary authority. In other respects the Restoration has been described as the Empire without Napoleon. Revolutionary and Imperial institutions were retained with very few changes. The administrative heart of the system, the Imperial council of state, became the king's council, with the same role of preparing legislation and providing professional training for the huge army of bureaucrats of which they were the apex. Ministers, all directly appointed by the king and individually, not collectively, responsible to him, had their own bureaucratic hierarchies, each appointing relevant officials, at all levels, throughout the kingdom. At the base of the pyramid were the 84 departments, new divisions carved out of the old provinces by the revolutionaries. Each was run by a prefect, appointed by the Minister of the Interior. Every official within this structure, down to the mayor and post-master of the tiniest commune, was appointed from Paris, on the advice of the local prefect. The Restoration retained the Imperial tradition of appointing outsiders as departmental prefects, although all other officials tended to be local men. Prefects acquired an even more important role in 1814 as electoral agents for 'suitable' deputies. The judicial and legal structures of the Revolution also remained in place. During the revolutionary years, a single centralised system of courts and standardised written codes of law had replaced the overlapping, jealously autonomous corporations and systems of law of the *ancien régime*. This centralised system was accepted in 1814 by all, except a small minority of *verdets*, ultra-royalists in western France, who dreamt of the restoration of a mythical de-centralised framework of semi-autonomous provinces.

A major issue in 1789 had been the problem of how to finance government. In 1814 the fiscal systems worked out during the Revolution were retained without question. These consisted of uniform direct wealth taxes, principally on land, but also on commercial, industrial or other business property. These were not taxes on income or profits as such; the *foncière*, or land tax, amounted roughly to a 16 per cent levy, while the *mobilière* and the *patente*, or industrial taxes, were concerned with the property on which business was based. These taxes raised less than one-third of the revenue the vastly expanded bureaucratic machine of government consumed. In 1804, detested old indirect taxes on salt, wine and tobacco were re-introduced to run local government and these *droits réunis* were maintained in 1814. The Bank of France, founded in 1800, also survived the Restoration, although the costs of war had put an almost insuperable strain on its reserves [196].

As sons of the Enlightenment, the revolutionaries had been committed to developing a lay, state system of education which under Napoleon became centralised. The Restoration retained the shell, but clerical control was gradually inserted into higher education, including the faculties and the more specialised *grandes écoles*. The Church regained dominance in the secondary schools, the *lycées* and the *collèges*, and in the managing body of the secondary system, the University, where in 1822 a senior cleric, Monseigneur de Frayssinous, became Grand Master. Primary schooling had never been taken out of the control of the Church [76].

The clearest indication that the First Restoration witnessed a continuation of the Empire was in personnel. Louis XVIII had spent his exile in the company of around 70,000 *émigrés* who expected that their sacrifice would be rewarded by jobs. Instead the king retained all those Napoleonic officials who were prepared to serve him. Louis kept 76 per cent of the Imperial civil servants, including 45 of the 87 prefects. Among the new prefects, 29 per cent had been Imperial prefects. In totality, two-thirds of the Restoration prefects had served Napoleon in a similar capacity [166]. Even the new Chamber of Peers, where *émigrés* may have expected to predominate, bore a close resemblance to the Senate. Only 37 senators lost their seats, 103 senators and marshals of the Empire sat in the new upper house.

THE HUNDRED DAYS

The king's circumspection was rewarded by a peace settlement that imposed neither an indemnity nor an army of occupation. However, France's borders were reduced to their 1792 position and she lost some colonies. This tolerable compromise was torpedoed by Napoleon's escape from Elba, a carelessly-adjacent choice of exile, just a short boat journey from Marseille. There, Napoleon was soon joined by sections of his old army and officials, apprehensive that the new monarchy would revert to old ways.

Thus ensued a 100-day resurrection of the Empire in which the federations that rallied were often more committed to the memory of the Revolution than Napoleon [35]. The Emperor was careful to revise his Imperial Constitution with Additional Acts, drafted by the doyen of liberals, Benjamin Constant. These mimicked the Restoration's parliamentary arrangements, declaring in their preamble that only the determination of the Allies to fight and destroy the regime had prevented Napoleon from establishing liberal institutions. Preparations were made to elect an assembly of 629 deputies by the 600 most wealthy males in each department.

The Allies had other ideas, convinced that a settled peace in Europe was inconceivable while Napoleon remained in power. His defeat at Waterloo heralded a very different Restoration, which soon began to show signs of 'impossibility'. The peace settlement drawn up in Vienna left all or part of 61 departments occupied initially by 1,200,000 Allied troops (reducing to 150,000) until an indemnity of 700 million francs had been paid. The 250 million francs annual cost of the occupation had to be borne by the occupied departments. France was now reduced to her 1789 borders, losing Savoy and some border fortresses. The Allies even demanded that the art treasures, gathered up by the Imperial armies, particularly in Italy, be returned. The British seized 75 Rubens and sent them back to their point of origin. Napoleon himself was exiled to the remote southern Atlantic island of St Helena.

THE WHITE TERROR AND THE SECOND RESTORATION

Parts of France remained in virtual civil war for several months after Waterloo, pacified only when the armies of occupation established themselves. Ultra-royalists in southern France, led by the comte d'Artois's eldest son, the duc d'Angoulême, did battle with the federations which had sprung up to defend Napoleon, and which subsequently were to be the nucleus of opposition to the Bourbons. A 'White Terror' was unleashed (the term refers to the white flag of the Bourbons), recalling the lawlessness of the early 1790s in which many were murdered, 200 Protestants in the Gard alone [67]. Thousands were injured, tortured, jailed or forced to flee. Houses and shops were ransacked and torched. In Marseille on 24 June 1815, the ultras inflicted 50 deaths, 200 were injured and 80 shops and houses fired. The Rhône valley was soon in uproar and the commander of the garrison in Toulon, marshal Brune, was assassinated in Avignon. In Nîmes, gangs, led by a labourer, Trestaillons, terrorised the Protestant elite. It was said they took down the women's drawers and beat their bottoms with a cudgel studded with nails in a fleur-de-lis pattern.

In Toulouse the ultra backlash was orchestrated by the *verdets*, so called because they wore the green cockade of the comte d'Artois. They even murdered the moderate royalist commander of the local national guard, general Ramel, when he tried to merge the guard and the *verdets*. They had no time for moderate royalism and were suspicious of Louis XVIII. The *verdets* dreamed of regional autonomy and a separate southern kingdom of 'Occitania', ruled by the unlikely and incompetent Angoulême. The violence recalled not only the conflicts of the 1790s, but the religious tensions of the sixteenth century in areas like the Languedoc where substantial Protestant communities had done well during the Revolution. Royalist local officials were either unwilling or unable to prevent the revenge attacks; Fouché's reputation as an omnisicient chief of police was shaken. Violence was brought to an end in the Var, Bouches-du-Rhône and Gard, three of the most disrupted departments, only by the arrival of the Austrian army of occupation. The White Terror was geographically limited. In Brittany during the Hundred Days, conflict between the federations and the royalist *chouans* had been restrained and counter-revolutionary reprisals were muted. In the occupied departments further north, the superior strength of the federations and the presence of foreign troops forestalled a violent ultra backlash [63; 167].

The unofficial White Terror was followed by an official purge. Talleyrand and Fouché, both too tainted with an Imperial past, were replaced in September 1815 by Richelieu, an efficient administrator, trailing a noble, landowning, *émigré* pedigree. A Chamber of Deputies of 402 members was elected in August. It was 90 per cent ultra and dubbed the *chambre introuvable* (unbelievable) by the embarrassed king. The deputies were bent on revenge for the Hundred Days; one member even demanded the death penalty for anyone who owned a tricolored flag. Emergency legislation gave prefects extra powers to maintain law and order and facilitated the arrest of anyone accused of plotting or publishing seditious literature. Up to 80,000 (one-third of all) administrators were sacked or demoted along with 15,000 army officers. The army was reduced to less than a third of a million men. The Chamber of Peers was purged of 29 members who had supported the Hundred Days. Over 70,000 political arrests were made. Special courts, (*cours prévotales*), were created to deal with the resulting prisoners, although only about 250 of the 6,000 subsequent convictions were their work. Lay courts imposed comparatively light sentences. Military courts were less forgiving. They ordered the arrest of 54 generals. Some escaped, but 17 were put on trial and some of the consequent death sentences caused a public outcry. The execution of marshal Ney in December 1815 turned him into a martyr for the liberals. While the White Terror may not have made the Restoration 'impossible', it certainly did ensure that a cohort of politically ambitious men were kept permanently alienated and excluded from public life. This was the very situation that Louis XVIII previously had sought to avoid [169].

2   SOCIAL TENSIONS

THE INHERITANCE OF THE REVOLUTION AND EMPIRE: THE RULING ELITES

Historians today focus on the political consequences of 1789 [72; 74]. During the years of the constitutional monarchy, observers of all political persuasions were very aware of the divisive social impact of the revolutionary years. In addition, the fashion for statistical reports on poverty of the 1830s, plus endemic social unrest, made people acutely aware of the social consequences of economic change. Cyclical economic depressions, occurring at roughly ten-year intervals, and always accompanied by peaks of social disturbances, completed a common contemporary view that society was in crisis as a consequence of class tensions [53; 65; 125].

During the Restoration, everyone, whatever their politics, was convinced that 1789 had been a bourgeois revolution, giving political power to wealthy, already established civil servants, professional men, especially lawyers and doctors, many of them substantial landowners. They secured positions in the revolutionary assemblies and in the vastly expanded bureaucracy. Nobles, on the other hand, had been accused as traitors, particularly those who emigrated with the royal family. The revolutionaries sequestrated land from heads of families who emigrated, noble and non-noble. However, Napoleon gave back unsold land to nobles willing to work for him, and they regained the rest in 1814. In total, nobles owned about 20 per cent of the land of France in 1814, 5 per cent less than in 1789. This was not as big a loss as Restoration ultras liked to assert in 1825 when they were negotiating (successfully) a state loan to compensate those who had lost land during the Revolution [92]. The electoral lists of the constitutional monarchy show clearly the continued dominance of nobles, who consistently were the largest landowners and the wealthiest men in the departments until 1848 and beyond [194].

Roughly one-third of Napoleon's senior bureaucrats, many of them nobles, had served the old regime. Many gained twice from the Revolution that had sought to dispossess them. They had received compensation from the revolutionaries for their loss of venal office, bought sequestrated land with the proceeds, and when the dust of the Revolution had settled, were appointed to official posts similar to those they had held before 1789. Napoleon also created a new hierarchy of titles and a legion of honour, elevating old nobles as well as his most successful generals.

In the second half of the twentieth century, revisionist historians began to dissect what was by then the prevailing republican orthodoxy that 1789 was an entrepreneurial, 'bourgeois' Revolution. They concluded that an elite of notables, part noble, part bourgeois, had been emerging during the eighteenth century. They argued that 1789 had made little contribution to this gradual change [72]. In their official appointments, economic interests and family ties, nobles and bourgeois might all be considered 'notables'. Indeed Napoleon had ordered his prefects to draw up lists of such 'notables' from which officials and members of assemblies could be selected. The qualifying factor employed was not birth, but degree of wealth and political compliance. Noble titles, of various derivations, were important qualifications for power during the Restoration. However, the litmus test of the Restoration elite was, like that of Napoleon, not nobility as such, but wealth and political preference [92]. Does this mean that there was a consolidated ruling elite in France in 1814?

We have seen that Louis XVIII retained as many of Napoleon's officials as he could, only dismissing them if they supported Napoleon during the Hundred Days. This would seem to support the idea that such a ruling elite existed, at a political level.

Bureaucratic dynasties were more and more noticeable [166]. The increased professionalisation of career structures for budding officials, educational prerequisites and hierarchical patterns of professional training, inherited from Napoleon, gave a sharper edge to the privilege of wealth. Even during the Revolution, the only men from poor backgrounds who could hope for the meteoric social advancement were the soldiers [*Doc. 3*]. In the Restoration the ambitious son of a noble *émigré* might have the best career prospects, but he was expected to climb the bureaucratic hierarchy from the bottom rung of the *conseil d'état* [63; 115; 194].

Restoration electoral law ensured that the nineteenth-century ruling elite was based not on quarterings of nobility, but on taxable wealth. Revolutionary and Napoleonic worthies were elected to

Restoration assemblies. The visible gradual growth of a market economy during the Restoration was indicated by the presence of bankers, businessmen and industrialists in local councils and in parliament. These groups accounted for 17 per cent of the deputies in the late 1820s, but, except in areas of rapid industrialisation such as Alsace, they were far less prominent than landowners, public officials and the legal fraternity.

Socially, there was no fusion. Old-regime noble families shunned Napoleonic nobles at Louis XVIII's court and similar exclusion was practised in provincial France, the memory of the 1790s making social prejudice all the more intense [39; 119]. In the view of the ultras, a bourgeois elite had insinuated itself into power which was motivated solely by financial gain and personal ambition. Ultras believed that it was their duty to arrest this perceived spiritual decline. Their champions were the comte d'Artois, who became king in 1824 and the Catholic Church.

THE INHERITANCE OF THE REVOLUTION AND EMPIRE: THE CHURCH

The most intractable tensions inherited in 1814 from the Revolution lay in attitudes to the role of the Church in French society. Before 1789 the Catholic Church had been the most privileged First Order, owning 10 per cent of the land. In 1814 the Church owned no land, all had been sequestrated during the Revolution. The clergy were paid civil servants, although bishops and archbishops were still drawn from senior noble families. The sense of grievance and outrage which the Church had experienced during the Revolution continued to reverberate through the nineteenth century. In 1814 the Church's biggest triumph was the statement in the constitution that Catholicism was the state religion of France. On the other hand, the constitution declared that the sale of Church lands in the 1790s was irrevocable. Future donations of property to the Church were permitted. From 1815 successive bands of young evangelical priests travelled through France, spending up to a week in a commune, urging the community to return to God, and in the process asking forgiveness for the Revolution. Their campaign included the public burning of anti-clerical books favoured by the revolutionaries, notably the works of Voltaire. Missionary crosses were ceremonially erected on communal, not Church, property, a clerical riposte to the trees of liberty that had been planted in the 1790s [75; 159; 189].

THE SOCIAL IMPACT OF ECONOMIC CHANGE

France was a nation of about 27 million at the end of the eighteenth century. 1801 was the year of the first full census and subsequently head counts were made every ten years, with updates at five-year intervals. The death toll of the Revolutionary wars was in the region of 1.5 million. This had the effect of slowing population growth. By 1815 the population was 29 million, 32.5 million by 1831, and 35.4 million by 1846. Other parts of Europe were increasing their numbers faster. The French accounted for 15.7 per cent of Europe's population in 1800 and only 13.3 per cent by 1850. There were few large towns. Paris was by far the largest and fastest-growing of French cities, containing 600,000 people in 1815 and over one million by 1846. Only four other towns had populations of over 100,000: Lyon, Marseille, Rouen and Bordeaux, and these were traditional regional capitals and commercial and industrial centres. But even collectively they were less populous than Paris. The rapid urbanisation of industrialisation, already visible in Britain, did not occur until much later, and only in very limited geographical areas, such as the north-east [53].

Actual population growth occurred in the countryside, with urban expansion merely a consequence of migration from rural areas. There were numerous traditional patterns of seasonal migration which assisted urban growth. Traditionally, adult males, of whom masons from the Creuse to Paris were one of the most visible groups, would leave their families as soon as the winter was over and work on building sites and lodge in Paris until the winter frosts stopped work. At this point they rejoined their families on their plot of land which the women, children and elderly relatives had been left to cultivate. Other characteristic patterns included young single adults leaving for a nearby small town, the girls usually going into service. In the half-century to 1850 some of this temporary migration gradually started to become permanent. A permanent drift began from the poorer areas of the south-west to Paris and the east and north-east. Although rural depopulation in the south-west was not perceptible until after 1850, as early as the 1820s economists were contrasting higher levels of literacy and prosperity in the north and east, compared with illiteracy, poverty and the dominance of the Catholic Church in the west and south-west.

The feature of these demographic changes which made most impact on contemporary observers was urbanisation, which is curious, given the tiny number of large towns. Towns were regarded as dangerous, sinful and unhealthy. This impression was reinforced by the cholera outbreaks of 1832 and 1848, which hit large towns, particularly Paris, far more severely than they impacted upon the countryside [108]. Ange Guépin, a republican socialist doctor in Nantes, was one of the first to make a detailed survey of the urban existence of the poor [*Doc. 4*]. His graphic account of the harmful effects of urbanisation on the health and morality of the poor was echoed by Dr Villermé in 1835 and Buret in 1840 [*Docs 5 and 6*], whose evidence was cited by Louis Blanc in his condemnation of capitalism. Novelists, memorably Eugène Sue and Victor Hugo, made their fortunes and those of the newspapers in which their stories were serialised with their versions of heartless, evil cities [*Doc. 7*]. Workers were encouraged, particularly by the saint-simonians, to write about their lives, in prose and poems. Suzanne Voilquin, Agricol Perdiguier and Nadaud were among the most famous artisans to be published and from them we have some impression of worker organisations and life [*Docs 8 and 9*].

By and large industrial growth was concentrated in the countryside. The exception was Paris, itself the fastest-growing industrial centre, focusing on the luxury trades. In 1814 France was the most industrialised nation in continental Europe, but still over 75 per cent of its people lived and worked in rural areas. The Revolution had abolished feudal dues and tithes and made many peasants sons of 1789. Over half of the land was owned by about six million peasant families, but many had holdings too small and too scattered to be able to sustain a family. The abolition of primogeniture, the right of the eldest son to inherit, merely aggravated the problem [135]. Many families were obliged to combine agriculture and craft industry, according to the season and the specific skills of individuals, or face penury. Most industry was artisanal, small-scale family enterprise, as can be seen by the fact that in 1851 only 3.7 per cent of the population worked in large-scale enterprises [139].

The immediate post-war years were difficult. The demobilisation of a large number of soldiers swamped the employment market. Production slumped in industries that had made uniforms and weapons. It became painfully apparent that the war had retarded economic growth in many areas. Britain was now seen as a dangerous competitor, able to export finished cotton, iron and also coal at low prices which French producers could not match. Producers successfully demanded protectionist tariff walls to defend their less advanced units. The silk and wine industries, which had dominated the European market through Napoleon's Continental System, thus faced the reciprocal tariff ripostes of France's neighbours. Until 1818 the government was obliged to concentrate its efforts on paying off the indemnity imposed by the Allies. In addition, the harvests of 1816 and 1817 were poor, leading to shortages and pushing up the price of basic foods. Popular disturbances, protesting against high prices and unemployment, became common.

From 1818 to 1826 the French economy experienced an economic upturn and gradual growth, to which government fiscal and commercial strategies may have contributed. An innovative branch of the cotton industry in Alsace began to install spinning machines in former monastic properties and a factory industry was born. Other trades remained firmly artisanal; however two significant changes started to impact, both on the economy and on social relations – the development of machines and changes in methods of production. Machines did not necessarily force workers into factories, but the cost of buying them reduced the independence of artisans, although they retained their own workshops and the appearance of autonomy. The silk industry was a notable example. In 1808 the Jacquard loom allowed a heavier, patterned silk to be woven, more able to compete with the new, fashionable, heavy embossed cotton. The new loom cost 1,000 francs, a fortune for weavers for whom three francs a day was regarded as a decent income. Weavers were forced to borrow and the most accessible lenders were the merchants from whom they bought their raw silk and to whom they sold the finished product. Weavers thus became economically dependent on merchants, who were able to break traditional agreements on prices and set terms advantageous to themselves. A similar form of proto-capitalism occurred in the cotton industry of Rouen. In neither case did a concentrated factory system develop [144; 157; 160].

Artisans in other trades complained that changes in methods of production were eroding their craft, and their livelihood. The development of 'ready-mades', *confection*, in tailoring, allowed the master tailor to 'put out' less skilled stages in production, tacking, etc., to cheaper, less qualified workers, usually women. Attempts to protect traditional skills and structures turned artisans into rebels in these years [104; 116].

In the countryside, the spread of the potato in northern France in the early part of the century increased available food supplies in the majority of years. Viticulture continued to expand, but Europe-wide protectionist tariffs cut markets, turning wine producers into critics of successive governments. Throughout the constitutional monarchy, years of bad wine harvest found wine producers out on the streets, attacking the offices of tax collectors, in protest against a fiscal measure which taxed the amount of wine produced, irrespective of its quality. Those who were producing for a more far-flung market were no less incensed because the high tariff policy followed by successive French governments throughout the period cut their export potential. Wine producers, rich and poor, had no time for the constitutional monarchy [102; 109; 121; 126].

Changes in the structure of the rural economy, launched by the Revolution and developed during the Restoration, also contributed to rural unrest. Revolutionaries had abolished feudal dues and with them permitted the sale of communal lands, if the commune agreed. The poorest inhabitants were the worst hit, being deprived of communal grazing and the use of timber from communal forests, vital for construction, tool-making and fuel. Protests became even more intense when the Forest Law of 1827 allowed the state, not the commune itself, to take possession of communal forests and sell them. The expansion of the iron industry, which mainly used charcoal for smelting, made timber a desirable and expensive commodity and one from which the state felt it should benefit. Attempts of peasants to preserve their communal rights became increasingly common. On countless occasions peasants 'invaded' former communal forests and took timber. Detachments from the local garrison frequently turned out to arrest them and gendarmerie reports sometimes recorded that the wrongdoer took his life in jail. In the detailed reports on the economy made by justices of the peace in 1848, the desperate problems caused by the sale of common lands were endlessly repeated [126; 170].

At the elite level, there were tensions and divisions during the Restoration, inevitable after the Revolution. They were exacerbated by the exclusion of some of the most active of Napoleon's officials after the Hundred Days and the attempt of Charles X to put the ultra myth of an aristocratic, clerical, monarchist elite into practice. But the conflicts among the notables were containable, because almost no one wanted another revolution. The social unrest among the poor was another matter, being more ubiquitous, disruptive and unpredictable in its consequences. It mirrored pressures over which the French had little control. Some of these pressures were driven by external factors like foreign competition and technological change. Climatic variations still interrupted the supply chain significantly; the 1816–17 harvest failures, which affected many countries, were apparently the result of a volcanic eruption on the other side of the world.

PART TWO: ANALYSIS

3 AN IMPOSSIBLE MONARCHY?

RESTORATION POLITICAL GROUPS

The White Terror polarised political groupings, roughly into liberal, royalist and ultra, though the lines of argument were never entirely precise. There were no formal political divisions in the parliaments throughout the entire constitutional monarchy; indeed politicians considered the idea of political parties as indicative of disloyalty to the regime. Groups coalesced around leading figures with patronage potential and were tiny or were very unstructured. The numerous contemporary biographical dictionaries of deputies during the Restoration tended to divide members into right, centre-right, centre-left and left as well as the ultra, royalist and liberal permutations with which historians are more familiar. Other, more colourful, labels were also applied from time to time by opponents. Ultras tended to think of liberals as Jacobins or revolutionaries.

Ultras

The ultras or ultra-royalists were even more royalist than Louis XVIII and were led by the king's brother, Artois, later to become Charles X. Although they dominated the *chambre introuvable*, subsequently they were never more than a vocal minority of 60–80 deputies, many drawn from southern and western departments. Ultras believed they stood for the traditional values of monarchy, Church and nobility, a trinity which they believed had once ruled France in harmony.

Beneath an apparent unity they were divided in their attitudes, not only to the Revolution, but also to the old regime. Some were anti-revolutionary and hankered for a return to what they imagined the pre-Revolutionary systems to have been. A minority wanted decentralised provinces managed by traditional elites. A larger number believed that a counter-revolution was needed [167]. The ideas of the latter group were typically developed in the writings of Joseph de Maistre and Louis de Bonald. They argued that deficiencies in the old regime led to the disasters of 1789. Ultras put more emphasis on the influence of the Church than more moderate royalists, but they were divided here too. Monseigneur de Quélen, archbishop of Paris and a typical ultra senior cleric, upheld royal authority and campaigned for ultra candidates in parliamentary elections. Gallicans favoured a French-centred Church. Ultramontanes, typically represented by the religious orders, especially the Jesuits, looked to papal direction. Ultras were of the view that traditionally royal authority had been seconded by a loyal aristocracy, overlooking repeated violent conflicts between nobles and the king in past centuries and ignoring the increasing divisions of various kinds – financial, social and political – among nobles themselves. Some ultras were grouped in the *chevaliers de la foi*, which had fought for a restoration during the Empire, others adhered to the *Congrégation*, a Jesuit-dominated secret society, active in Restoration politics. Others followed the respected writer, Chateaubriand, despite the fact that his campaigning for a freer press aligned him at times with the liberals [40; 91].

Royalists
Between 1816 and 1827 the vast majority of members of the Chamber of Deputies belonged to no group at all and would have simply thought of themselves as royalists. They would have defined themselves as constitutional royalists, loosely united in their acceptance of the Bourbons and keen to make the Charter work, not because it represented the triumph of 1789, but because it conformed, in part, to the aspirations of the notables before the Revolution. Depending on the occasion and the individual, they would align with ultras or liberals [162]. The changing balance in the Chamber between liberals and ultras was as much due to individuals realigning themselves as actual changes in the individuals elected. The ultra backlash after 1820 pushed a number of constitutional royalists, such as Casimir Périer and Guizot, towards a more resolutely liberal stance. Historians tend to divide the Restoration years into blocks of time dominated successively by ultras or liberals. However, except for 1815–16 and 1827–30, the groups on either extreme depended on an amorphous centrist block of royalists who were committed to keeping the system afloat and avoiding the radicalism of the ultras or the left.

The Left
A variety of names were appended to men who later came to be known as liberals. There were doctrinaires, constitutionals or 'independents'. These groups were just as imprecise as the ultra and royalist

labels. In a broad sense the left were thought of as the heirs of 1789 and the Empire, but that inheritance encompassed a wide range of political preferences. Many liberals had bought *biens nationaux*, property confiscated from the Church and nobles during the Revolution, in the 1790s, were anti-clerical and suspicious of ultra backing for the Church. The ultra stampede for jobs after Waterloo caused 'independents' to fear that the 'bourgeois' gains of 1789 were being obliterated.

Most left-wing critics of the restored monarchy were convinced after 1815 that a monarchy was the only viable form of government [*Doc. 10*]. In contrast to what might be expected, very few were overtly republican or Bonapartist. A sustained sense of loyalty to the Emperor remained, as the Hundred Days had shown. This loyalty extended beyond the military. However after Napoleon's death in 1821 there was no suitable heir. His young and sickly son was brought up in the Austrian Empire and his mother, Marie-Louise, repudiated any links with France. Bonapartism thus became a somewhat sentimental patriotic memory, sustained by secretly-circulated memorabilia and songs sung in cafés by maudlin veterans after a few jars. Many former revolutionaries were convinced that Napoleon had saved the Revolution. However the fact remains that the Empire had never provided a satisfactory solution to the problem of how to govern the country. The revised constitution of the Hundred Days had done little to convince politicians that a constitutional, rather than an autocratic, Empire was possible. Napoleon's own memoirs, written on St Helena, in which he claimed that he had been forced by belligerent foreign adversaries to rule as an autocrat, succeeded in convincing few other than his nephew, Louis-Napoleon.

There were two generations among the liberals. There were older men who had served the Revolution and/or Napoleon. Those who were dismissed, or denied promotion after the Hundred Days, formed the fulcrum of resistance to the Bourbons. Resistance was particularly strong among Napoleonic officers retired on half-pay in 1815. Then there were young men, at school during the Empire. A family tradition of republicanism/Bonapartism emerged with the Cavaignacs and Carnot, son of the regicide, as notable figures. A cohort of young people, born between 1792 and 1803, began to study medicine, law or in the specialised colleges like the *école polytechnique* in the early 1820s. They listened to Guizot and Victor Cousin [*Doc. 11*] and took common cause against the clericalism and dubious constitutionalism of the Restoration. As children of the Romantic Age, they believed that they could change the world [186]. Established and wealthy liberals, particularly in Paris and eastern France, encouraged a younger generation and underwrote minor rebellions. They included men like Voyer d'Argenson, one of the richest and most idiosyncratic radicals and a member of an illustrious noble family that had served the *ancien régime*. An important influence in Alsace were the Koechlin brothers, cotton manufacturers who bought former monastic property to house their new machinery and were always ready to support a radical cause [36; 147].

Clandestine Organisations

Clandestine groupings were intrinsic to both right- and left-wing politics. Liberals included conspiracy as well as social and political reform in their armoury. These were not necessarily conflicting liberal 'tendencies'. Many individuals moved successively through the whole gamut, with some emerging after the 1830 revolution as revolutionaries, some as socialists and some as distinctly conservative supporters of the Orleans monarchy. Nor was conspiracy an exclusively left-wing preoccupation. There was a tradition of secrecy in Catholic formations, in freemasonry, which was sometimes left-wing, sometimes conservative, and in the *confraternités* and *compagnonnages* organised by the various craft industries [180; 193]. Secrecy was in part dictated by the Civil Code, article 291 of which demanded that any association of more than 20 members should apply to the local prefect for permission and supply him with a list of members, rules and where they met. This forced all opposition organisations underground throughout the whole period of the constitutional monarchy.

The ultras led the way with the *chevaliers de la foi* during the Empire and the *Congrégation*, a clandestine Catholic brotherhood which was rumoured to have considerable political clout during the Restoration [167]. Radical secret societies sprang out of the federations of 1815 and freemasonry, including the *chevaliers de la liberté* in western France, centred on the cavalry school of Saumur and the *Union*, begun by the lawyer Rey in Grenoble and Paris. Rey's Bonapartist rhetoric attracted notable liberals like Lafayette. In 1816 his attempt to seize Grenoble in the name of a republic with about 4,000 men, many of them Napoleonic veterans, came to nothing. Twenty-five of his supporters were executed after a trial designed to convince critics of the futility of opposition, but to no avail. In Paris the radical Bonapartist masonic lodge, the *Amis de la verité*, started by Joubert, Bazard and Buchez in 1818, soon had 1,000 members, almost all young medical or law students [36; 147; 168].

Liberals and ultras inevitably had opposing attitudes to the Revolution, but sometimes co-operated in attacking royalists, on press censorship and election laws in particular. It would be wrong to say that the ultras and liberals were two consistent and consistently active polarised forces. Both groupings were loose associations pushed into a semblance of coherence by circumstances.

AN 'APPRENTICESHIP' IN PARLIAMENTARY POLITICS

Louis XVIII was intent on avoiding further foreign travel, as was Richelieu. In September 1816 the *chambre introuvable* was dissolved, and the excesses of the White Terror were curtailed. Ultras had far less influence in the new Chamber, numbering only 90 out of an assembly reduced to 258 members. A new electoral law, the Lainé law, proposed by the liberals, ordered that in future one-fifth of the Chamber should be renewed annually. This was to guard against the dramatic swings of mood that had led to the *chambre introuvable*. In the election of 1819 the ultras were reduced to 40 and the independents were strengthened by the election of 55 deputies, including Lafayette, Constant and Manuel. In 1818 Richelieu was replaced by a member of his own government, Decazes, a moderate royalist with an Imperial past [98].

THE BOURBON ARMY

The structure and organisation of the army was a contentious issue. Before 1789 the French state was protected by regiments of professional soldiers, including Swiss and other foreigners. The conflicts at home and abroad during the next quarter-century necessitated a mass conscript army. Napoleon's successful campaigns created regiments with profound loyalties. Louis XVIII was keen to disrupt these loyalties and despite his tolerance in other directions, he had not hesitated in ordering the restructuring of regiments on a departmental basis. 1814 had witnessed the immediate retirement of a substantial proportion of the officer corps. The Hundred Days, in which the military had been quickest to respond to the Emperor's appeal, ensured an even sharper purge after Waterloo. The *émigrés* had no desire for a professional conscript army, but promoted the idea of a volunteer body run by noble officers in a tradition of privileged service. The result was division and weakness.

In 1818 the liberal Minister of War, the former Imperial marshal Gouvion St Cyr, introduced legislation which, although it caused fierce divisions in parliament, laid the basis for the army of the future, both conscript and professional. It was agreed that 40,000 men would be recruited to the ranks annually by lot, to which all 20–year-old males were subject, although those with enough money could buy a replacement. Recruits would serve for six years. The rich could buy a commission and set their own terms. To ensure that the officer corps had a professional, not merely a privileged ethos, all prospective officers had to serve for two years as NCOs, or graduate from one of the two military colleges, to which entry was by competitive examination [*Doc. 12*]. Some of Napoleon's officer corps were brought out of retirement to make up numbers. They experienced profound frustration when inexperienced young nobles were inevitably promoted over their heads. Imperial loyalties remained deeply-rooted and it was not by chance that the support for the *charbonnerie* and the conspiracies of the early 1820s came predominantly from the army, particularly from the junior officers and NCOs, frustrated by limited promotion prospects compared with those under Napoleon [95; 171].

Whatever foreign policy the Bourbons had pursued would have seemed tame after the massive expansion of French territory during the Empire. Their actual achievements should not be underestimated. The indemnity was paid off by 1818 and the Allied occupying troops withdrew. France was admitted to the re-named Quintuple Alliance, whose aim was to sustain co-operation between the Great Powers, and consequently, a balance of power. A parallel Holy Alliance, devised by Tsar Alexander I, was an association of monarchs determined to combat any whiff of liberalism or revolution. A series of congresses was held. At Aix-la-Chapelle in 1818 France joined the Alliance. Further meetings of monarchs to discuss how to handle revolutionary disturbances took place at Troppau, Laibach and Verona between 1820 and 1822.

As a consequence of their debates, the Austrians kept themselves busy containing insurrection and liberal ideas in the Italian peninsula and parts of the German Confederation. Spain was left to the French. In April 1823, the French government sent an army of 100,000 men to help the Spanish king to defeat his liberal challengers. The success of the operation helped to promote loyalty to the Bourbons within the army, perhaps because any military campaign was better than life in a departmental capital, where the chance of promotion was very low. Military uniform became fashionable at court, the royal family established close links with the military college at St Cyr and even the duchesse d'Angoulême acquired a military boyfriend. The French also supported Allied backing for Greek independence from the Holy

Roman Empire. Colonial developments were not forgotten, climaxing in a successful campaign in 1830 in Algeria. Nonetheless it was always the left which could wave the flag of patriotism, condemning the right for its emigration, and unfairly, for the defeats of 1814–15. Patriotism was an unswervingly left-wing commodity [82].

THE PRESS

Another controversial issue was press freedom, promised in article 8 of the Charter of 1814 [*Doc. 2*]. It was a 'freedom' which had been typically honoured and truncated during the revolutionary years and as in so many other aspects, the Restoration followed the revolutionary tradition. During 1817 and 1818 the emergency laws against sedition passed in 1816 were relaxed and a lively combative press began to emerge. The ultra press encompassed the *Quotidienne*, the *Gazette* and the *Drapeau Blanc*. The leading liberal paper was the *Constitutionnel*, which had 20,000 subscribers in 1826 and included both the young Thiers and the more staid Casimir Périer among its writers. The most distinguished liberal paper was the *Courrier*, which, despite its modest subscription list of 6,000 names, was edited by the senior liberal thinker, Benjamin Constant, and the politician, de Broglie. The paper with the second largest circulation was the *Journal des Débats*, initially founded by the ultra campaigner for press freedom, Chateaubriand, but with the liberals Guizot and Royer-Collard among its contributors.

At 70–80 francs for an annual subscription, national daily papers were mainly bought by wealthy notables who composed the *pays légal*. Thus they were an incomparable mouthpiece through which to speak to the voters. Local newspapers were cheaper, although they tended to avoid controversial political issues. Through cafés and the ubiquitous *cabinets de lecture* (reading rooms), one newspaper could reach many more less wealthy readers. Repressive press laws, prohibitively high caution money demanded of editors (a deposit paid by editors before they were allowed to publish) and repeated prosecutions for 'political' offences, affected both a popular and an elite readership. Juries were notoriously reluctant to convict editors, however inflammatory their language. The issue of press freedom created an unlikely alliance of ultras and liberals, who, together, founded the Society for the Freedom of the Press in 1818. As a consequence, press censorship was relaxed in the Serre laws of 1819, devised by the Minister of Justice, de Serre, in consultation with de Broglie, Madame de Stael's son-in-law, and Guizot, then employed in the Ministry of the

Interior. This legislation narrowed the scope of censorship. The test became that a paper could only be prosecuted if it could be shown to have actually provoked an illegal act, itself a hard case to prove. Future prosecutions had to be heard by a jury. Caution money was abolished [47; 115; 154].

THE POLARISATION OF POLITICS IN THE 1820s

An assassination, the work of one totally insignificant individual, was seriously to disrupt the fragile, but functioning and broadly welcome, political equilibrium. In February 1820 the duc de Berri, son of the future Charles X and next in succession to the throne, was murdered. The assassin, Louvel, was a saddler, whom the ultras quickly declared a liberal, but who had no previous political role and no connections with opposition groups. However, the ultras used the opportunity of the murder as an excuse to attack the liberals, capitalising on the Europe-wide revival of liberal claims and conspiratorial strategies.

In direct response to the assassination, the outraged ultras managed to push the control of politics to the right. Richelieu re-emerged as Chief Minister. De Serre was retained, but he shunned his former liberal allies and policies. Habeas corpus was suspended for three months, facilitating the imprisonment of suspected conspirators without trial. Press censorship was intensified. Caution money was reinstated and several newspapers, liberal and ultra, were forced to close. Most controversial was a new electoral law, the 'law of the double vote'. The Chamber of Deputies was increased from 258 to 430 members, the additional 172 to be chosen in special departmental electoral colleges by the quarter most wealthy voters, who would thus exercise a double vote. Liberals were outraged and some ultras, who believed that a much wider electorate would be more royalist, also opposed this blatant intensification of the domination of a wealthy elite.

From the early 1820s, and particularly, when he became king, Charles X made a conscious effort to appoint members of old, particularly *parlementaire*, families in all branches of public service, the army, the Church, the judiciary, as well as the prefectures. Those who were passed over for promotion were inevitably resentful. Restoration politics were shaped into a caricature of the social conflicts of the 1790s. The stark delineation in prefectoral reports and other government documents became a conflict between a landed royalist aristocracy and bourgeois liberals, however nonsensical this was in reality [166].

THE *CHARBONNERIE*

The move to the right provoked lively resistance, at first concentrated in the secret societies, but gradually occupying a more public arena, as the illegality of government's strategies began to leave radicals as the only credible defenders of the constitution. The *Amis de la verité* organised demonstrations against the law of the double vote in 1820. They hoped, in vain, that their protest would attract widespread support. Subsequently the main leaders fled to Italy to evade police scrutiny. There the conspiratorial tradition was nourished by professional revolutionaries like Buonarroti, a survivor of Babeuf's abortive *Conspiracy of the Equals* of 1796, a democrat, a republican and a believer in the radical re-distribution of property. The French exiles, Joubert and Dugied, were drawn to the *carbonari*. This was a secret society, based in Naples, that honoured the ideals of 1789, including the tricolour flag. Its name evoked the isolated life-style of charcoal-burners. It was organised in tiny cells or *ventes* (a term used in the timber industry to mean 'new growth'). On their return to Paris in 1821 they began to organise a French *charbonnerie*. It quickly spread throughout eastern and south-eastern France in areas where traditional radicalism had been sharpened by the presence of occupying troops. The *charbonnerie* attracted upwards of 60,000 members in 60 departments.

The *charbonnerie* was split into cells of 20 or fewer, so that it could evade the Code. Its clandestine ceremonies, symbols and oaths were similar to those of freemasonry and journeymen's associations. The cells were often based on the local garrison, or clustered around a number of Napoleonic veterans. Many affiliates had fought with the federations in 1815. It also attracted artisans and was financed by the liberal elite, including Voyer d'Argenson and Lafayette. Members were instructed to arm themselves and several small plots, based on different military garrisons, ensued: Lyon in 1819, Belfort in 1821, neighbouring Colmar a few months later, and culminating in the plot of four sergeants stationed in La Rochelle in the first weeks of 1822. In each case the plans for a rising were abortive, the most active plotters seem to have been police spies, paid by results, but the nervousness of the regime when faced with subversion within the army led to harsh reprisals. The four sergeants were executed [168; 171; 185].

The involvement of the army in Spain seemed to mark a turning point. Some French liberals fought for their Spanish counterparts, but the regiments sent to Spain remained loyal. Subsequently, in France the wave of conspiracies ceased and the *charbonnerie* faded. Why? It has been suggested that the army preferred overseas activity to service in provincial towns in France [152]. It may be that the execution of conspirators convinced radicals of the ineffectiveness of insurgency, although in comparison with Louis-Napoleon's repression of republicans in 1851, Restoration governments were fairly lenient. However, the conspiracies and the *charbonnerie* never had precise goals, beyond a pronounced loyalty to Napoleon and his death in 1821 eliminated a Bonapartist alternative [185]. From the end of 1822 radical affiliates of the *charbonnerie* began to focus on social and political reform [147].

SOCIAL REFORM: THE SAINT-SIMONIANS

In the early 1820s, social commentators, first in England, then in France, began to compile statistical assessments of poverty, unemployment and low wages, especially among women. Social theorists began to dream of ideal worlds. The most original of these was Charles Fourier, a travelling salesman who hailed from Besançon, who argued that contemporary 'civilisation' denied human nature and should be replaced by 'harmony' [*Doc. 13*]. His new society would consist of *phalanges*, autonomous communes of about 2,000 members, where everything would be shared: work, sex, children, as well as profits. He believed that the liberation of women from monogamous marriage through education and job opportunities, was the first step in social regeneration. Fourier's first book, *Four Movements*, appeared in 1808, but the bizarre nature of some of his ideas and language, meant that few read him until the 1830s and then many expressed horror both at his feminism and his praise of sexual licence [43; 79; 165]. These aspects of his theories were popularised, with little acknowledgement, by another unusual group of social reformers, the saint-simonians.

This sect, or 'church' as it called itself, was formed by some former members of the *charbonnerie*. They had sought a more specific focus for their humanitarian ideals and found it in Saint-Simon. From the early 1820s he popularised plans for the regeneration of society. His espousal of what he called 'New Christianity' shortly before his death, was somewhat ironic for a man who, in 1789, had renounced his famous ancestry and made and lost a fortune in *biens nationaux* in a life of extravagant dissipation. Students, particularly from the *école polytechnique* and the medical schools, were attracted to his theory, taken in part from the English economist, Adam Smith. He postulated that society was basically divided into *oisifs* and *industriels*, idlers and workers, the second a broad category including everyone who had to work at something to survive. He held that the political world should be re-shaped to put government into the hands of the *industriels*.

After Saint-Simon's death in 1825 his disciples grouped themselves into a saint-simonian movement, dedicated to the liberation of workers and women, the two groups perceived as the most excluded from contemporary society. Under the leadership of Prosper Enfantin, Rodrigues, Michel Chevalier and others, they publicised their theories in the *Globe*, edited by Pierre Leroux, and by 1829 had embarked on campaigns to attract workers and women into their movement and to take practical steps to educate and house these excluded groups [51; 97; 120; 131; 149].

POLITICAL REFORM: THE DEFENCE OF THE CHARTER

The new direction of government policy meant that liberals could criticise the Restoration without pursuing conspiracy. Opportunities for entirely legal criticism were afforded by the government's erosion of the 1814 constitution. The law of the double vote was a crude panic measure to smother opposition. It was assumed that the richest voters would elect the most right-wing deputies. To some extent, the prognosis was realised in the sweeping victories of the right between 1822 and 1824, but in 1827, and more particularly in 1830, even the 'double vote' constituencies were precarious as 'safe' seats. The calculation that wealth meant conservatism was disproved by an analysis of members of parliament. In 1827, 38 of the deputies who paid more than 3,000 francs in tax were considered left-wing, while only 19 were on the right. If the legislation palpably failed to secure its concrete objectives, it did help to create a unity and sense of direction which the left-wingers had previously lacked. The left could begin to claim, with justification, that they alone were the defenders and champions of the constitution, and that royalists were trying to emasculate it.

Government election strategy allowed the liberals to assume the moral and legal high ground. In 1820 prefects were ordered to maximise the royalist vote. Officials were instructed to order their subordinates to vote for government candidates, if they wanted to keep their jobs. Prefects were told to compile lists of the richest, most influential voters in each constituency and to instruct the men on this list to put pressure on other voters in the constituency, who often depended on the notables for their livelihood. Thus was launched a sustained campaign which soon led to 'virtual' elections. Government cheating was made easier by the absence of a formal procedure for renewing electoral lists. The onus was on voters to prove they paid enough tax to qualify. Prefects perfected a variety of tricks to exclude liberals. Some would announce that the list was to be revised, but they would display the list in a position where no one could read it, or disappear until the final few minutes of the revision period, making it impossible for liberals to prove that they qualified for a vote. Some tried to disenchant liberals by imposing all the jury service on them, but this was a dangerous strategy, leading to the acquittal of those accused of press offences. Prefects were unscrupulous in excluding qualified liberals and sometimes even including royalists who were not qualified, or who had died. Between 1820 and 1827 this cheating was so successful that the total number of electors fell from around 100,000 to 79,000. Prefects falsified the results as well as the lists. Unsurprisingly, in the 1820 elections for the new departmental colleges and replacing the fifth of the assembly due for renewal, the liberals were left as a rump of 80, the rest of the seats being shared between royalists and ultras [105].

Pressure for a more right-wing orientation to politics increased during 1821. Royalism seemed on the ascendant, reinforced when the widow of the murdered duc de Berri obligingly produced a 'miracle child', Henri, duc de Bordeaux, an heir for Artois. Richelieu's press laws were assailed by liberals and ultras at the end of 1821. Nagged by his brother, the king appointed a government dominated by Artois and the ultras and led by the comte de Villèle, a former member of the *chevaliers de la foi* and mayor of Toulouse during the White Terror.

The star of the ultras was undoubtedly in the political ascendant. In the first partial renewal of the Assembly in 1822, Voyer d'Argenson and Lafayette, life-long champions of liberal causes, lost their seats. In March 1824 liberals were reduced to 19, and in September the ultras acquired their own champion as king Charles X. This dramatic reversal of political fortunes was partly a response to optimism about the economy and was partly in support of French policy in Spain, but the main factors were the 'double vote' and the government's manipulation of electoral lists and results.

The right continued to clamour for its favourite causes – the Church and the problem of land lost during the Revolution. First however, the new Assembly tried to protect its own political future by yet another change in the constitution. The partial renewal of the Chamber each year was replaced by a general election every seven years, in a *loi septennale*. The Assembly then declared that the new law could be applied retrospectively.

RELIGION AND THE RIGHT

Religion was one of the most divisive issues of the Restoration, not because liberals were irreligious, but because they retained their anti-clericalism from the revolutionary years. The increased penetration of the clergy into the lay secondary and tertiary education system alarmed liberals. In 1822 Monseigneur de Frayssinous was made Grand Master of the University. The popularity and influence in the faculties of leading liberals like Guizot and Victor Cousin was challenged. Faculties were shut down for extended periods, liberal professors were dismissed and replaced by clerics [101]. In 1825 the 100 ultra members of the *chevaliers de la foi* in parliament organised a law against sacrilege which made 'profanation of the host' a capital offence. Although the law was never implemented it was seen by liberals as further evidence of the advance of clerical power [87].

The coronation of Charles X in 1825 was an ostentatious public indication of the advance of clerical influence. Louis XVIII had been crowned at Notre-Dame, Charles preferred an elaborate pseudo-medieval pageant at Rheims cathedral, apparently evoking memories of Clovis and a romanticised past. The new king became intimately linked to the Church, to the extent that he was frequently caricatured in clerical dress. The connection was intensified by the use of the clergy as electoral agents. As early as 1822, under the influence of the future Charles X, bishops were asked to use their pulpits to promote the election of ultras. The practice became increasingly common in the elections of 1827 and 1830 [*Doc. 14*]. The organisation of a state loan to indemnify *émigrés* whose lands had been confiscated during the Revolution, a highly controversial piece of legislation passed in 1825, was a further demonstration of the political clout of the ultras. Liberals argued that the indemnification called into question the permanence of the revolutionary land sales and was a waste of 600 million francs of state cash, but the legislation was speedily implemented, visibly benefiting families who had no need of charity.

THE CONSOLIDATION OF THE LEFT

Both the law against sacrilege and the indemnification loan served to unite formerly very disparate radical critics. However, it was the government strategies in elections and in intensifying press censorship which gave the radicals an identifiable cause, the defence of the 1814 Charter. The two pivotal organisations were the *Société des Amis de la Liberté de la Presse* and *Aide-toi, le ciel t'aidera*. The former, an alliance of ultras and liberals, successfully campaigned against Villèle's attempt to increase press censorship. Although the proposals were accepted by the Chamber of Deputies, in the Peers, the powerful voice of former Imperial nobles and ultras, including Chateaubriand, led to rejection. The Peers were punished by the nomination of 76 new (and it was hoped) tractable members.

Aide-toi, set up in 1827 under the presidency of François Guizot, a moderate liberal committed to the Restoration, focused entirely on the conduct of elections and the composition of electoral lists. It put pressure on the government to establish rules for the annual checking of electoral lists. The *Globe* newspaper served as the headquarters for *Aide-toi*, which mushroomed out from the initial committee of 20 in Paris, to small groups in each department. It circumvented legislation on associations because it claimed to be a temporary formation, involved only on elections. It was run by men who had been in the federations and the *charbonnerie*, many of whom were both deputies and lawyers. It was careful to keep within the law and to make its brief the observation of the law. It sent out a series of leaflets, starting with 80,000 copies of a *Guide to Voters*, explaining how to prepare the necessary documentation to ensure that those who qualified appeared on the electoral lists. Other pamphlets described how an election should be conducted, and what to do if voters suspected that cheating had occurred.

Liberal pressure over elections was such that in 1827 the government was forced to bring in a set of rules on the revision of electoral lists. The reinstatement of 25,000 excluded liberals on voting lists and a similar bolstering of the lists of potential candidates (clipped by nearly a quarter since 1820) soon brought the lists back to 1820 levels. The scale of the liberal campaign was such that in 1827 Villèle became so apprehensive that he might lose his majority if he delayed the election that he recommended that a general election be held that autumn, while he still had a chance of winning. He miscalculated. At least 180 liberals were elected, about the same number of royalists and about 60 ultras. *Aide-toi* challenged the conduct of the elections in 22 departments and the courts upheld their accusations of cheating in ten cases. Villèle faced the prospect of numerous by-elections provoked by liberal allegations, and thus the likelihood of liberal victories. He chose to resign.

Very properly, in accordance with the customary practice of tailoring ministries to majorities in the Chamber of Deputies, Charles accepted Villèle's resignation and appointed a centre-right government, led by Martignac, a member of the old administration. Royer-Collard, one of the liberal chiefs, was appointed president of the

Chamber of Deputies. Aware of his precarious role in this hung parliament, Martignac tried to please both extremes. Legislation to exclude unrecognised teaching orders, principally the Jesuits, was followed by a reduction in the caution money demanded of newspapers and a plan to make local councils elected, instead of government-nominated, bodies. Ultras welcomed the dilution of centralisation, but the proposal to limit the vote in local elections to the quarter-most-rich, aroused the liberals to a new campaign to abolish the law of the double vote itself. The king ordered Martignac to kill the bill.

ECONOMIC CRISIS, 1827–32

Meanwhile Martignac had taken steps to address the economic crisis that had been developing since 1827. This crisis was caused by a number of factors. It was at once a traditional food crisis, the result of consecutive poor harvests, of grains, grapes and potatoes, and also a commercial and industrial recession set off by financial uncertainties and increased bankruptcies. Wheat prices rose 50 per cent above the norm and remained high until 1832, when harvests recovered. Potatoes and bread were staple foods and by the winter of 1828 bread prices had risen from 11 to 21 sous for a standard 4lb loaf. This created serious problems for the poor. A price of 13 sous represented an expenditure on bread of 50 per cent of an average wage. Coupled with persistent wage cuts, underemployment and unemployment for artisans, this was a serious crisis.

Marches and demonstrations, demanding government action, became common in the artisan districts of central Paris. As always, the government was criticised for its fiscal policies, notably the *droits réunis*, indirect taxes paid by the producer on wine, salt and tobacco. It was reckoned in some areas in these years that wine sold for less than the tax due. Those who produced export-quality wine joined silk manufacturers in criticising high tariffs imposed on foreign goods, iron, coal and cotton in particular. On the other hand, the producers of iron, coal and cotton goods argued for higher tariffs to keep out foreign supplies.

Martignac took the unusual step of organising government enquiries into both the wine and iron industries, in which producers and others were asked why they thought their trade was depressed. The official conclusion was that the Continental System of the First Empire had encouraged over production and that it was down to producers to work together to slim their industries. The enquiries raised the hope that the government would assist in some way. However, no consensus was reached as to what was the best strategy to overcome the problems. A sliding scale was introduced to allow grain to be imported, but as few foreign producers had much by way of a surplus, this did not help. Reports of peasants halting convoys of grain and selling it at a 'fair' price became common. The enquiries fruitlessly politicised the crisis. Wine producers needed no encouragement to bombard the government with petitions for a revision of the tax system. The lack of official response intensified accusations of official culpability.

In the past Marxist historians saw the economic crisis as a cause of the 1830 revolution. There is no doubt that popular unrest among artisans and peasants increased, but it was very varied in objectives, diffuse and sporadic, and alone would not have brought down the regime. Marxists also used to be adamant that 1830 was a second-wave 'bourgeois' revolution. It is true that it became customary for prefects, especially those who were new to an area, to report that the 'commercial and industrial middle classes' were liberal to a man. While interest groups tried to put pressure on the government to raise tariffs, decrease taxes, etc., the messages were contradictory. Silk producers were opposed to protectionism, iron masters wanted tariffs on imported iron increased. Some cotton producers in less advanced areas like Rouen wanted a tariff wall, others in areas using more modern methods like Mulhouse were ready for the wall to come down. There was no unity among the commercial and industrial middle class on economic policies. On the other hand, liberal manufacturers were as apprehensive as any ultra at the threat of popular riot and disorder. In some respects therefore the economic crisis made the risk of political conflict within the elite less intense [127; 146].

4   THE 1830 REVOLUTION

WHY WAS THERE A REVOLUTION IN 1830?

The Three Glorious Days, as the 1830 revolution was called, occurred at a point when a prolonged economic crisis and a quite unconnected political crisis coincided. To what extent does this juxtaposition explain the revolution?

At a purely political level, the 1830 revolution was the consequence of the polarisation of politics after the succession of Charles X, but it was not a simple conflict between the two extremes, ultra and liberal. Successive right-wing governments were rendered powerless by the growth in liberal numbers and by the presence on the extreme right of ultra critics, one section of whom, led by Chateaubriand, were willing to ally with the liberals to prevent legislation going through. Although the rival groups had very different attitudes to the recent past, the crisis of 1830 was more the product of mutual fears, suspicions and ignorance than fundamental cleavages and radically opposing objectives. Ultras claimed liberals were revolutionary, liberals described ultras as enemies of the constitution. While both allegations contained elements of the truth, almost no liberals wanted a revolution and virtually no ultra wanted an absolute monarchy.

The Martignac government resigned in August 1829, having failed to steer any of its legislative proposals through parliament. If he had followed customary practice, because most of the by-elections since 1827 had gone to the liberals, the king should have appointed a left-of-centre government. Instead, he nominated an assortment of ultras, including his close friend, the prince de Polignac, then ambassador in London. The prince was a diplomat with no experience of parliamentary politics, yet in November he was made Chief Minister. The re-call of parliament was postponed from December to March. Liberal newspapers, including the *National*, launched in January 1829 and edited by Adolphe Thiers and Mignet, vociferously condemned the appointment of a government which could not possibly gain the confidence of the deputies. *Aide-toi* deputies and their newspapers organised banquets and a petition in which signatories agreed to refuse to pay taxes until such taxes were voted by parliament.

In his speech from the throne in December 1829, Charles attacked the liberals and demanded support for his government, making it difficult to separate monarch from ministers. (To add to this, there were rumours that Polignac, son of one of Marie-Antoinette's favourites, might have been Charles X's son.) Traditionally parliament responded with anodyne support. However on this occasion the Chamber of Deputies, insisting that they were totally loyal to the king, passed a motion of no confidence in the government, 221 deputies supporting the motion [*Doc. 15*]. On 19 March Charles dissolved parliament and then alarmed liberals when he delayed for two months before calling a new election [*Doc. 16*]. During this time the liberals fêted the '221' as popular heroes. *Aide-toi* held all the aces. Prefects were shuffled around departments as the government desperately tried to gain support.

On 23 June, the election took place in the individual constituencies (*arrondissements*) into which each department was divided, and on 3 July in the special departmental electoral colleges in which the richest 25 per cent had a second vote. In 20 departments liberals refused to accept the proposed electoral list and the voting was delayed. In total, 270 liberals were chosen, including 202 of the 221, and 145 royalists. The government's defeat was all the more remarkable when the proportion of deputies holding official posts, 'place-men', is considered. In 1828 it was reckoned that of 1,500 men who had sat in parliament during the Restoration, 1,180 held official positions.

THE FOUR ORDINANCES, JULY 1830: A ROYAL *COUP D'ETAT*?

Charles regarded the results as a challenge to his own authority. After some argument, he and his Chief Minister decided to activate article 14 of the Charter [*Doc. 2*] which allowed the king to make decree laws in 'an emergency'. The electoral defeat was described in these terms. On 25 July the king issued the Four Ordinances, or decree laws, from his palace at St Cloud, justifying them on the grounds that the liberals, especially their newspapers, were a revolutionary threat to the security of the regime [*Doc. 17*]. The first ordinance simply withdrew all surviving aspects of press freedom, ordering all critical papers to cease publication, or risk the seizure of their presses by the police. The second dissolved the new assembly, before it had even met. The third called new elections for early September, and the fourth disenfranchised 75 per cent of the electorate, leaving only the 'double vote' electors to vote for a Chamber, which was itself reduced to 258 members. The remainder of the electorate were merely allowed to propose candidates. These royal decrees were published in the official *Moniteur* on 26 July [*Doc. 18*].

In agreeing to the ordinances, Charles behaved more like a sleep-walker than a decisive embryo-autocrat. His actions have been described as the 'suicide' of the Bourbons. An anonymous cartoonist showed Punch (the king), assaulting the Charter (Judy) [*Doc. 49.1*] and even a sympathetic historian described the ordinances as a royal *coup d'état* [3]. Charles seemed genuinely to have been convinced by ultra advisers that compromise with the liberals was impossible. It is true that Charles was an *émigré* ultra with limited knowledge of the revolutionary years and their impact, but, until August 1829, ultras, royalists and liberals had muddled along tolerably well. Why did political crisis turn to revolution?

If it had been left to the educated political elite, it was quite likely that the ordinances would have been absorbed, with grumbling resignation, into the political game. Liberal unity collapsed as the crisis turned to revolution. The liberal newspapers were most immediately at risk and 44 editors and journalists met and agreed to publish a written protest at the illegality of legislation decreed without the consent of parliament [*Doc. 19*]. However they could not agree to defy the first ordinance, so some never published the protest. The most radical paper, the republican *Tribune*, did not bring out an edition. The two largest liberal papers, the *Constitutionnel* and the *Journal des Débats*, followed suit. In the event it was the more moderate papers, those which had hinted at the desirability of an Orleanist monarchy, such as the *National*, the *Globe* and the *Temps*, which published the protest of the journalists. Thiers, representing the *National*, played an influential role in composing the document [*Doc. 20*].

What turned a political crisis into a revolution was the intertwining of hesitant elite mutterings with more robust popular protest. This was facilitated by the geography of central Paris. The central artisan districts, which were home to the luxury trades of the capital, such as tailors, hatters, shoe-makers, cabinet-makers, metal workers, printers, etc., had been in a ferment of demonstrations and protests for three years in reaction to the economic crisis. The Four Ordinances drove more men and women than was usual on to the streets for one of the Monday demonstrations (there was a tendency to extend the weekend Sunday break by another day). The usual crowd was joined by the print workers and journalists, made unemployed by the new decrees. What made their turbulent marches dangerous was that the central artisan quarters also contained the newspaper industry itself and adjoined the centres of government. Close by were the town-houses of nervous liberal deputies. The streets in which they demonstrated were narrow and easy to barricade. Careful military planning would be needed if the effervescent situation was to be contained.

The king must have known that the ordinances would be interpreted as the *coup d'état* the liberal papers had been predicting for a year or more. Yet he had made no plans to bolster the forces of law and order. Ordinary minor infringements of law and order were in the hands of the local police commissioners. During the 1789 Revolution a volunteer civil militia or National Guard quickly developed, the nucleus of which was usually made up of former soldiers, the bulk being small businessmen and artisans. It was an uncertain ally for those in authority, and after 1815 remained a symbol of the Revolution, playing an ambiguous role during the Restoration, keen to maintain law and order, but a bastion of Bonapartism. This ambiguity culminated in the dissolution of the organisation by the king in 1827, following a royal inspection, that was accompanied by shouts, the most polite of which was 'Long live the Charter'. This meant that if a civil disturbance threatened to get out of hand, the authorities could not rely on the Guard, and there was a danger, which indeed occurred during the 1830 revolution, that former guardsmen would dig out their uniforms and weapons, and fight with the insurgents [*Doc. 21*].

For the authorities, their best hope of controlling a major disturbance was to call out the local regiment of the gendarmerie. Unfortunately for Charles X, in January 1830 a substantial force had set off for Algeria, taking Algers on 5 July, but leaving the capital without reserves. The king put Marmont, duc de Raguse (1774–1852), in charge of the defence of Paris. Marmont had been a Napoleonic marshal. He had deserted to the Bourbons in April 1814 and this had allowed the Allies to enter Paris without a struggle. It also gave the French language a new word for traitor, *ragusard*. Marmont had never received the rewards he had anticipated. He had become the military dustman, the habitual choice for controlling civil unrest. For instance, he had been called into the situation in Paris in 1827. This ensured that he was deeply unpopular with a wide section of Parisian opinion in 1830. In theory, Marmont had 13,000 men at his disposal, half of them his own Royal Guard. In practice, he could never muster more than 6,000. The available line regiment was so jealous of the privileged Royal Guard that many deserted in this new crisis to the rebel side [*Doc. 22*] [3; 146; 159]. Initially, Marmont remained sanguine because in 1827 he had controlled the unrest with a much smaller body of men.

THE THREE GLORIOUS DAYS

The revolution began on 27 July, with the erection of barricades at several points in central Paris, but Marmont was so confident that the situation was under control, that he sent his men back to their barracks in the suburbs at nightfall. On 28 and 29 more substantial barricades were raised and manned in the right-bank artisan districts, near the Hôtel-de-Ville, the rue Saint-Honoré, the Palais Royal, the Tuileries, St Antoine etc. [*Doc. 49.2*]. Marmont was helpless. Men in National Guard uniforms and his own officers and men deserted to the opposite side of the barricades [*Doc. 23*].

On 29 July the royal troops abandoned the Tuileries and with this the fighting was effectively over. No accurate figures exist of the numbers of dead and injured. Some sources claim that as many as 2,000 people were killed. Others put the figures lower, with 800 insurgents and 200 soldiers killed. The figures for the injured also vary, with the highest total standing at 4,000 rebels and 800 soldiers. About 1,750 of the 6,000 soldiers deserted to the rebels. Most of the dead and injured among the insurgents were young, skilled artisans.

The artisan combatants looked to the liberal journalists and deputies for leadership, apparently unaware that by and large these were mere fearful onlookers to the struggle. It was only on 29 July that the deputies, after frantic and indecisive meetings, sometimes at Périer's home, sometimes at the house of the Orleanist banker, Laffitte, finally published a timid criticism of the Four Ordinances, in which they insisted on their loyalty to the king. Only 41 of the 73 deputies present actually signed the document [*Doc. 24*]. Anxious to assert themselves, after they had realised that the king was losing control and the initiative was passing to Lafayette, who had been commander of the first National Guard in 1789 and was now the champion of the Parisian artisans, some liberal deputies and journalists, especially Thiers's cohort from the *National*, declared a 'provisional municipal committee' at the Hôtel-de-Ville. It was composed of moderates, Orleanists, republicans and Bonapartists, and included Casimir Périer, Jacques Laffitte and Mauguin [*Doc. 25*].

Late on 29 July, Charles, who had stayed at St Cloud, apparently unaware of the seriousness of his position, agreed to dismiss Polignac. That night Thiers placarded Paris with posters recommending Louis-

Philippe, duc d'Orléans, as a more effective head of state than Charles. The Orleanists were using the crisis to press their own agenda. The next day, on the urging of some of the deputies, Thiers went to Louis-Philippe's home at Neuilly to offer him the role of lieutenant-general of the kingdom. On 31 July, persuaded by his sister that Charles X was a spent force, Louis-Philippe returned to the capital to accept the lieutenant-generalcy and to take part in a staged procession to the Hôtel-de-Ville with Lafayette. Dramatic reconstructions show Lafayette embracing the duke on the balcony and wrapped in tricolour flags. Captions claim that Lafayette apparently hailed the duke's elevation as 'the best of republics'. Even in the late twentieth century, historians describe this episode as symbolising Louis-Philippe being accepted as a future ruler by the artisans at the Hôtel-de-Ville before he was appointed by the deputies [98]. Charles abdicated on 2 August, leaving the throne to his grandson, the duc de Bordeaux, aged seven, but acknowledging Louis-Philippe as lieutenant-general during the minority. The king then fled to England through an unresisting and unsupportive countryside.

1830 IN PROVINCIAL FRANCE

The virtual self-destruction of the Bourbon regime was a Paris affair. The departments had their own 'July Days'. These only involved sustained violent confrontation in a few cities, notably where Bourbon officials tried to resist, such as in Nantes. In 1830 the departmental revolutions consisted of the local liberals, usually at the head of their *Aide-toi* committees, taking over the running of the department. Bereft of news from the capital after the arrival of the Four Ordinances until early August, the departments became, in the words of one justice of the peace, 'little separate republics'. The lead was taken by the recently elected liberal deputies, Imperial officials dismissed at the Second Restoration and former National Guard officers. Often the liberal take-over was facilitated by the fact that the prefect had returned to his home district to vote, and as it was summer, had not promptly returned to his post. Where he was present, the liberals either secured his consent to their seizure of power, or chased him from the *chef-lieu*, the main town in each department. It was not unusual for members of the judiciary, led by the government prosecutor, as in Besançon, publicly to declare the Four Ordinances illegal. In Bar-sur-Aube the prosecutor cleared the courtroom of the bust of Charles X and draped an enormous tricolour flag over the fleur-de-lis wallpaper. The failure of officials to speak up for the Bourbons and the escalation of popular demonstrations against the regime sharpened the ambitions of local liberals [*Doc. 26*].

The economic crisis had already provoked grain riots and attacks on tax offices. The absence of a firm lead after the news of the ordinances, created the opportunity for the less well-off to protest further, demand tax changes and sing Bonapartist or republican songs. Wine-growers were prominent in demonstrations against the hated indirect tax. On 2 August, wine-growers in Besançon wrecked the tax office. The revolution encouraged people to assert their traditional right to timber from communal forests. In Lyon, where four days of demonstrations by artisans, notably joiners, had occurred a month earlier, prisoners in the jail mutinied and workers took over the *hôtel-de-ville*.

Local liberal notables showed no more sympathy for popular unrest than had the Bourbons. They hastened to set up provisional administrative committees and National Guard patrols to maintain order. The presence on the streets of marching National Guardsmen, brandishing tricolour flags, signified both their radical patriotism, and formed a bulwark against the escalation of popular violence. This was particularly important because the other guardian of public order, the gendarmerie, was tainted by its association with the Bourbons. Attempts in Dijon, Besançon, Nantes and other cities to use troops against rioters were disastrous, leading to increased violence. In Metz, junior officers and men sacked their colonel and declared for the revolution. In Lyon, a wiser military commander made himself head of the liberal provisional committee.

Both notables and poorer people in provincial France were quick to produce posters and petitions demanding a change of regime. The ubiquitous tricolour flags which appeared were often inscribed 'Long live the Charter'. Several cities in the east, including Strasbourg and Besançon, declared for a republic. Anti-clerical attitudes mingled with patriotic slogans. A focal point for popular demonstrations was the demolition of the recently erected missionary crosses and their replacement by trees of liberty. The liberals in the small Jura commune of Arbois chased their *curé* out of town. In some cases the political crisis was a smoke-screen behind which personal scores could be settled. Popular anti-clericalism was most manifest where the local bishop was a leading ultra, as in Paris, Nancy and Besançon. In Nancy on the night of 30–31 July, artisans ransacked the cathedral and the seminary. The seminary's furniture was burned. Unrest often occurred when a local priest refused to bless tricolour flags.

Rioting workers and peasants were notably absent from departmental provisional committees. In the Puy-de-Dôme, typically, seven out of the 15 members were lawyers. Liberal landowners, doctors, businessmen, drawn from an older generation as well as from a different economic background, combined to prevent unrest spreading and shared out local jobs among themselves and their friends. Many claimed jobs from which they had been ousted after the Hundred Days. The committees systematically replaced officials at all levels, often breaking tradition and appointing one of their number as prefect, as well as nominating sub-prefects, mayors and police chiefs. If possible, the most senior local official disgraced at the Hundred Days was made prefect. They put pressure on Bourbon officials to resign and when the news that a new monarchy had been declared was announced, they underlined their decisions by organising the preparation of thousands of multi-signatured petitions of loyalty to Louis-Philippe. The committees completed the local revolution in mid-August when they sent lists of the newly-appointed officials to the new Minister of the Interior, Guizot, who simply rubber-stamped them. Thus although changes at the centre in 1830 were the work of Paris, the departments transacted their own revolution [90; 146].

5   ORLEANISM: WHAT WAS CHANGED BY THE 1830 REVOLUTION?

Orleanism was invented in the wake of the 1830 revolution. The main emotion uniting the liberals was fear that the revolution could escalate out of control. Thus a hastily concocted revision of the 1814 Charter was prepared. The recently elected parliament, which had never met, was quickly assembled. On 3 August the two Chambers met and agreed, in the space of one afternoon session, very modest constitutional changes. Only a minority of either House actually turned up; 252 deputies, of whom 219 voted to revise the Charter; 114 of the 365 Peers appeared, 89 accepting the changes. On 7 August parliament declared that the throne was vacant and offered it to Louis-Philippe, who took the oath as king two days later [*Doc. 27*].

LOUIS-PHILIPPE, KING OF THE FRENCH PEOPLE

How was it that the demise of the Bourbons led to the appointment of the king's cousin in his place? Charles, through a mixture of indecision and unrealistic assumptions, manoeuvred himself into a corner from which the only exit was abdication. The liberal deputies did not want to remove him, merely influence his choice of ministers. They did not even want to dictate who should be in the government. They made as few changes as possible to the Charter. Why did the deputies choose Louis-Philippe? The duc d'Orléans, who had been an *émigré* with his Bourbon cousins, had returned to France the richest man in the kingdom, the biggest beneficiary of the indemnification of 1825. He was a loyal supporter of the Bourbon monarchy, unwilling to acknowledge the idea of an 'Orleanist alternative' which his banker, Jacques Laffitte, and a handful of friends dreamt up in 1827. It became common in the late 1820s to compare Louis XVIII with Charles II of England, Charles X with James II, and infer that France had her equivalent of William of Orange waiting in the wings. Louis-Philippe would never have stepped out of the wings willingly. He was part of the Bourbon Establishment. Had Charles X survived as king until his death in 1836, Louis-Philippe would have been the obvious choice as regent to rule until the 'miracle child' was old enough. He was made king in August 1830 because of his proximity to the deposed monarch. That he was chosen is an indication of how non-revolutionary most of the liberals were.

However a revolution had occurred and the tiny Orleanist faction had contrived to push their candidate forward. It was important to dress the duc d'Orléans up as the choice of the 'people', to make this conservative manoeuvre look radical. Thiers reminded everyone that Louis-Philippe had fought with the revolutionary armies at Jemappes, and forgot the rest of his life. An amazing range of slogans was invented to sell his cause. He was called a republican/bourgeois/citizen king, even 'the king of the barricades'.

Louis-Philippe's supporters praised his 'bourgeois' life-style. His Paris home, the Palais Royal, had been turned into a business by his father, and the son continued to exploit the shops, cafés, theatres and whorehouses which filled the buildings surrounding the enclosed courtyards of the palace. He took his walks through this thriving and fashionable community, carrying the quintessential symbol of bourgeois respectability, a rolled umbrella. His sons went to the local *lycée*. His wife was religious. He was the devoted father of a numerous brood, in contrast to the licentious life of the Bourbons, including Charles X in his youth. His numerous portraits, always showing him in his National Guard uniform, were in marked contrast to the old-world pomp of the paintings of Charles X [122].

However it was all a manufactured image. Louis-Philippe represented continuity, not innovation, political or social. Why were the deputies so lacking in adventure? Some were known to have strong Bonapartist loyalties, but *l'Aiglon*, Napoleon's son, was too sick, too young, too foreign and too far away to take seriously. Why not a republic? Some, for instance Mauguin, had republican leanings, republicans took a vociferous lead at the Hôtel-de-Ville, and republican groups emerged during the July Days. The liberals who took charge in 1830, the leaders of *Aide-toi*, argued that only a small minority preferred a republic and that any attempt to proclaim one would have led to civil war and the risk of foreign intervention to maintain the 1815 settlement.

Although artisans, journalists and students manned the barricades in 1830, they had no common political voice, merely specific, mainly economic, grievances that at first they hoped the liberal politicians would address. It was the more conservative of the liberal deputies who pushed themselves to the fore and seized control. Their hurried settlement was accepted because no one wanted to risk a re-run of the 1790s. The fate of the democratic republic set up after the 1848 revolution showed how divided were republicans. The idea that France's new Allies, the other four Great Powers, might intervene on behalf of the Bourbons, was not far-fetched, given the record of the so-called Congress Powers in Italy, Greece, Spain, and of course France itself in 1815.

However, when the oaths taken by Charles X in 1825 and Louis-Philippe in 1830 are compared, it is clear that, although the new king was closely related to the old, the deputies intended that he should never forget that he owed his throne to them [*Doc 28*]. He would always be a 'king of the French people', never 'king of France'. The setting for the oath-taking on 9 August underlined the shift from a monarch with divine-right pretensions to a king appointed by a group of self-assembled parliamentarians. There was none of the pseudo-tradition devised by Romantic ultras, no minutely planned elaborate cathedral coronation, simply an oath taken at the Chamber of Deputies, surrounded by massed National Guardsmen and their banners. Speed, not style, epitomised the occasion [59].

THE CONSTITUTIONAL CHARTER, AUGUST 1830

The main differences between the Charter of 1830 and that of 1814 were that the ultra preamble was removed, as was article 14 [*Doc. 29*]. New article 13 specifically denied the king the right to suspend or dispense with existing laws. The right to propose new laws was given to deputies and peers as well as the king, and the right of the deputies to vote tax changes was reinforced. Curiously, the issue of ministerial responsibility, the extent to which parliament could influence the choice of ministers, was left as ambiguous (article 12) as it had been in 1814. The Chamber of Peers was modified. The voting age was reduced to 30 years and that of candidates to 35 years. In 1814 the king had promised, in a sacred oath, to defend the Charter. In 1830, in addition to the king's promise to parliament, the Charter was entrusted to the 'patriotism and courage of the National Guard and all French citizens'.

Under the 1830 Charter, Catholicism was no longer the official religion, but merely that of 'the majority', which, combined with the promise that lay education would be expanded, was an indication that the liberals intended to live up to their anti-clerical past. Freedom of expression and the total end of censorship were promised. A final paragraph listed future legislation, including jury trials for press and other political offences, the obligation to seek re-election for deputies who were given an official post, the election of National Guard officers and local councils, and the abolition of the double vote. A new electoral law was also promised.

The 1830 Charter was a quick fix and no one's ideal constitution. The Restoration liberals had reluctantly sunk their differences in the late 1820s to defend the constitution and oppose Polignac, but liberalism had no ideological substance. The decision to invent an Orleanist monarchy based on a constitution which, with a few notable exceptions, confirmed the 1814 settlement was the work of the most conservative of the liberals. They put it about as a compromise, a *juste milieu*, a middle way to avoid conflict. In reality they allowed no time to formulate compromises and their subsequent determination to maintain the 1830 Charter almost as a Holy Grail was interpreted by critics as the selfish clinging to power of a small wealthy elite [40]. The minimal scale of constitutional revision suggests that the Restoration was only an impossible regime to historians determined to prove that France was destined to be a republic [169].

The new constitution was passed by 246 votes to 12. All officials and parliamentarians were asked to take an oath of allegiance to the new king and constitution; 99 deputies refused and resigned. A total of 110 by-elections was held in October and they marked the demise of the tenuous liberal unity; one-fifth of the new deputies were radical critics of the new government. Only the more conservative of the liberals were satisfied with the constitutional revision. They had soon won the name 'resistance', in comparison with the 'movement', who wanted more radical changes. Criticisms ranged from demands for a substantially wider electorate and a popular vote on the constitutional revisions to the call for a new assembly empowered to devise a completely new constitution. A few critics demanded social reform to help the poor, particularly tax revisions.

One of the most visible differences between the Restoration and the Orleanist regime was the proliferation of elections. National Guard officers were to be elected by universal male suffrage. In April 1831, 200-franc taxpayers were given the vote in parliamentary elections. The total electorate grew to 166,000 and by 1846 stood at 240,000. The vote was also given to less wealthy *capacités*, members of Academies and other institutions of note, if they paid 100 francs in tax. This honoured a liberal notion that voting required 'capacity', which, it was argued, could be equated with intelligence and judgement and not merely wealth. The resulting electorate, five in every

1,000 Frenchmen, was liberal in comparison with the rest of continental Europe, where elected assemblies were still the exception, but narrow compared with Britain where the 1832 Reform Bill gave the vote to 32 men in every 1,000. The French electorate remained predominantly a landowning elite, as did the Chamber of Deputies itself, where the tax qualification for membership was halved to 500 francs and the age limit reduced from 40 to 30 years.

In 1831 municipal councils were made elective, as were departmental and *arrondissement* councils two years later. The change made little difference to their composition. Although the electorate for these local councils was the same as those for parliamentary elections, in order to have the minimum prescribed number of voters in each constituency, in poorer departments those who paid 80 francs or less were enfranchised. The actual electorate tipped two million, almost a quarter of all adult males [32; 124].

What did all these elections signify? The National Guard elections were either neglected or in some towns republican opponents were habitually elected, leading to the dissolution of particularly recalcitrant battalions. Abstention rates were high in elections for local councils, partly because it was recognised that departmental and *arrondissement* councils had a very limited role. Municipal councils had more of a say in people's lives and left-wing critics gained control of some towns. The constitutional nature of the state was confirmed, but parliament had no more of a voice in the choice of ministers than before 1830 [42; 111].

SOCIETY: WAS 1830 A BOURGEOIS REVOLUTION?

On the face of it, the most radical change of the Orleanist period was the abolition in December 1831 of hereditary right to membership of the Chamber of Peers. Future life-peerages were to be awarded by the king to reward loyal public servants. The law stated that the qualification for membership was a certain number of years of public service: six years for deputies, ten for prefects. Louis-Philippe continued to include peers in his governments, and a substantial proportion of the lower house was still drawn from peers of all sorts. However, ambitious politicians were reluctant to accept a life-peerage, particularly as it came without a pension. The law did not abolish the hereditary peerage as such. No more hereditary titles were conferred, but those that existed continued to have substantial social clout, even though their members were denied access to the upper house. Indeed, the peerage was so attractive that families continued to invent titles.

The abolition of the principle of heredity in the upper house contributed yet another name for the regime, the bourgeois monarchy, which implied that 1830 had been a social revolution. Orleanists revelled in their status as members of the bourgeoisie. 1830 was portrayed as the continuation of the social revolution of 1789, progress to an open society, career open to talent, the end of traditional privilege and the predominance of the bourgeoisie. This was just advertising fudge. The social basis of the Orleanist regime was little different from that of the Restoration; the rule of a wealthy, predominantly landed elite which exploited official patronage to the full. In this context, both, and neither, were 'bourgeois' regimes. 1830 did not elevate a new ruling class; it confirmed the power of already established families, whose influence often pre-dated 1789 and whose prestige had barely been touched by Charles X's theatrical attempts to 'revive' noble power. Nobles continued to figure prominently in government, admittedly most of them sported Napoleonic titles. It is true that some legitimists temporarily 'emigrated to the interior' in 1830, refusing to take the oath to the new king and thus losing official jobs. But this withdrawal was short-lived and within a few years legitimists were standing for, and being elected to, parliament, and continuing to dominate in the regions [194]. Contemporary socialists like Louis Blanc [*Doc. 30*] shrewdly commented that 1830 was a bourgeois revolution not because it brought the middle classes to power, but because it confirmed their already well-established position and failed to acknowledge the modest claims of those who had fought on the barricades.

A generation later, Karl Marx put a quite different spin on the story of social revolution. He was convinced that ownership of the means of production determined economic change and that society was destined to move through successive stages, aristocratic landed, to entrepreneurial bourgeois, to a proletarian and finally to a classless society. In this context he claimed that 1830 put power in the hands of an elite of bankers and businessmen. Conveniently, two out of three of the first Chief Ministers appointed were bankers. That was the beginning and the end. In fact, the number of businessmen in the Chamber actually fell from 17 per cent before 1830 to 14 per cent after. In the 1830s and 1840s social commentators criticised the uncomfortable social consequences of industrialisation, but economic change was relatively slow in France compared with Britain. Blanc was nearer to the truth. Despite the publicity about the bourgeois regime, France was still run by a traditional bourgeoisie, not a new entrepreneurial middle class.

LA RÉVOLUTION ESCAMOTÉE: WHATEVER HAPPENED TO THE ARTISAN REVOLUTION?

Etienne Cabet, the Orleanist politician who later became a socialist, dismissed 1830 as 'une révolution escamotée', smuggled away from the real revolutionaries, the Parisian artisans [*Doc. 31*]. Artisans expected that the new government would solve their economic problems. Instead, the July Days led to a predictable intensification of the economic crisis. The 1830 harvest was disastrous, after an unusually cold winter. Demonstrators hoped that the new regime would make major social reforms, including the abolition of indirect taxes on wine, salt and tobacco. Some of the new Orleanist prefects anticipated reform and suspended the collection of the tax on wine. Only very modest reductions were introduced and some emergency grain imports were permitted in 1830. The next two harvests were no better and in 1832 subsidised, sometimes free, bread and reduced price grain were distributed if there was a risk of serious popular disturbances.

The Orleanists showed no more enthusiasm than their predecessors to intervene to try to reverse economic trends in a systematic, permanent fashion. Liberal economists like Sismondi were convinced that the national economy should be self-regulating. The public assertion of economic liberalism ran in tandem (and in contradiction) with protectionist tariff policies established during the Restoration and demanded by major producers. Economic crises, like that in which the July Days occurred, continued to be muddled through with a combination of private and municipal charity. Charity workshops, *ateliers de secours*, similar to those set up in the 1790s, were cobbled together from August 1830, under the pressure of escalating popular demonstrations, providing jobs for 3,000 in Paris. By December at least 10,000 unemployed were clamouring for help. The government was obliged to increase and extend its loan to Paris. Six years later the city was still trying to pay back the money. The economic crisis deepened during the winter of 1830–31 and in March 1831 the Périer government was forced to institute a detailed enquiry into the economic health of the nation. As a consequence, central government funds were used extensively in departmental relief programmes in 1831 and 1832. The scale of the problem can be seen in the example of the small commercial city of St Dizier. In February 1832, 75 per cent of the workforce was dependent on the municipal workshops [127; 146; 150].

Thus the Orleanist revolution satisfied only part of the Restoration liberal opposition and almost totally failed to address the economic crisis. Small wonder that the new regime experienced more unrest in its first five years than had its predecessor in fifteen.

6 THE RADICAL RESPONSE TO THE ORLEANIST REVOLUTION

Popular unrest, already a common feature of the economic crisis in town and countryside, escalated markedly after the July Days, sometimes in minor incidents, sometimes in the rebellion of a whole city, and was to remain a constant problem until after the second rebellion of France's second city, Lyon, in April 1834. The episodes of unrest focused on economic issues, particularly tax reform, anti-clerical demonstrations, demands for patriotic action, and attempts to influence political decisions, for instance the demand that Charles X's ex-ministers should be punished. The response of the Orleanists to the demonstrations of the 'popular classes' was military repression. The situation was stabilised mainly by economic recovery, for which the government could claim no more credit than they deserved blame for repeated cyclical crises. Political radicalism was a direct product of disillusion with the absence of political and social reform. The worst nightmare of the *résistance* was realised with the rapid fusion of elite and popular criticism.

THE TRIAL OF THE EX-MINISTERS

The incarceration of four of Charles X's ex-ministers in the Vincennes fortress added another element to artisan demonstrations about wage cuts and price rises. The insistence of liberal politicians that the Four Ordinances caused the July Days led to popular pressure that those responsible should be put to death as retribution for the deaths of so many 'July heroes'. Reluctantly, the new regime agreed to a trial and the investigating process began to arraign the four before the Chamber of Peers on a charge of treason. There were additional fears that legitimists (the name now applied to all Bourbon supporters) might try to persuade the Allies to reinstate Charles. National Guard units and Odilon Barrot, prefect in Paris, seemed more sympathetic to the demonstrators than to the more temporising approach of the government. The more conservative 'resistance' ministers, Guizot, de Broglie and Périer, resigned in protest at the end of October, leaving the more radical 'movement' leader, Laffitte, to head an otherwise not noticeably more left-wing government.

December 1830 was a very dangerous month for the new regime. The trial of Polignac and his associates was due to open on 15 December at the Luxembourg palace, close both to the effervescent artisan district of Saint-Antoine and the no less excitable *école polytechnique*. The funeral of the liberal thinker, Constant, took place on 12 December in the Protestant chapel in the rue Saint-Antoine, accompanied by popular demonstrations and demands that he should be interred in the recently restored secular shrine of the 1790s, the Panthéon. The National Guard commander, Lafayette, was put in charge of both the 50,000 guardsmen and the 30,000 soldiers. Although the trial was carefully orchestrated, large demonstrations calling for the death penalty took place. The danger that substantial detachments of the guardsmen might rebel when the ministers were merely condemned to life imprisonment was narrowly averted. Louis-Philippe paraded through Paris accompanied by Lafayette and his men. Within a few days Lafayette, an icon to the artisan and student crowds, had been transferred to a merely honorary position in the National Guard, and resigned in protest at this lack of gratitude [98].

ANTI-CLERICAL RIOTS

Anti-clericalism played a major role in popular unrest. It was a direct response to the evangelical campaigns of the Restoration and the political activities of well-known ultra clerics, such as the archbishops de Quélen, of Paris, and Rohan-Chabot, of Besançon. Where there were substantial Protestant communities, rival gangs re-ran age-old conflicts. In the Gard at the end of August, seven were killed in such clashes [67]. Ultra clerics went into hiding. In Paris, the archbishop's palace was sacked; vestments and sacred books were flung into the river. Similar scenes occurred in Nancy where the seminary had been a base for the evangelical campaign, and where the bishop, Forbes-Jansen, was a leader of the *Congrégation*. Priests were bullied to fly tricolour flags from church towers, to bless National Guard standards and say prayers for the new king. When they were not compliant, ugly scenes could result. Rumours abounded of priests gathering together to discuss the prospects for a third Restoration. In the following months anti-clerical outbursts became increasingly common.

The main targets were missionary crosses, put up in recent years by evangelical priests. They were pulled down, often carted to the local church, sometimes set on fire and replaced by the radical favourite of the 1790s, trees of liberty. In what was frequently a carnival atmosphere, the tree-planting was accompanied by the singing of banned revolutionary songs, the 'Marseillaise', 'Ca Ira' or the 'Carmagnole'. Colour was added with flurries of tricolour and, occasionally, red flags, and a *bonnet rouge* would often be put on the top of the tree. Music and more colour was added in the uniforms of the National Guard, usually flanked by local officials, the mayor, government prosecutor, sometimes the prefect, giving the occasion an air of official sanction. The local officials who took part were typically former Bonapartists, out of office since 1815. At first the Parisian response was tolerant, then embarrassed, and finally sharply critical of these processions, partly because so many local officials joined in and partly because the majority of demonstrators were artisans. After the seminary in Nancy was looted on the first of several occasions in July 1830, those arrested included five workers in the cotton industry, four shoe-makers, a painter and a carter.

The peak of popular anti-clericalism was the sacking of the church of Saint-Germain l'Auxerrois in central Paris on 14 February 1831 after a memorial service for the duc de Berri. During the Restoration such services were customary and some were held in 1831 without comment. The plan for a large service at the church of Saint-Roch, next to the Louvre, was abandoned on the advice of the prefect of police, but the *curé* of the nearby Saint-Germain l'Auxerrois agreed to offer a substitute venue. The service was attended by 150 leading legitimists and terminated with the placing on the catafalque of a portrait of the duc's son, Henri, together with a crown of leaves, the leaves then being distributed among the congregation.

Later that day the church, along with a number of others in the capital, was wrecked. The archbishop's palace was left uninhabitable. Twenty of the congregation were arrested, but acquitted of conspiring against the regime. Rumours of legitimist plots floated a new wave of popular anti-clerical incidents through France. In Dijon, excited crowds surrounding a new tree of liberty shouted 'Long live the Republic!'. The performance at the local theatre, always a barometer of the political temperature, was delayed as gangs of youths waved tricoloured flags to the rhythm of revolutionary songs [146].

PATRIOTISM AND NATIONAL ASSOCIATIONS

Liberals all claimed to be patriots in the 1820s. It was quickly apparent after the July Days that they meant different things when they spoke of patriotism. The more radical among them had a more proactive view and were eager to help liberal revolts abroad. The more conservative liberals were apprehensive that France's former enemies might see the July Days as a reason to restore the Bourbons yet again.

A rash of national associations for the defence of French territory appeared in the early months of 1831. Apparently, inspired partly by fears that legitimists, in league with foreign powers, threatened a Bourbon coup, they were also eager to offer fraternal support to insurrection in Belgium, the Italian states and above all, Poland. The Belgians revolted against rule by the Netherlands in August, the Poles revolted against their Russian masters in November 1830. Both appealed to the French, the Poles recalling the contribution of Polish soldiers to Napoleon's campaigns. While the Paris government took a cautious line, Lafayette presided over the Polish committee in Paris, as did the senior president of the royal court and government prosecutor in Metz. Even the more conservative 'resistance' wing of the Orleanists (so-called because they resisted change) were for the Poles, but support for the Belgian revolt was more confined to the radical 'movement'. The volunteer battalion bound for Brussels was put together by General Lamarque, Bonapartist veteran, Restoration liberal and supreme commander of the army in western France since the July revolution. *Aide-toi, le ciel t'aidera*, almost as much at odds with the new as with the old regime, collaborated with the newspaper, *Le National*, to support Lamarque's efforts.

In February and March 1831, rival defence committees were set up in Metz. The most active was the group run by the *mouvement* which canvassed door-to-door. Local radical newspapers carried the idea to other eastern cities and a week later, on 14 March, when a new government, headed by the staunchly *résistance* Casimir Périer was announced, Parisian newspapers also promised to publish lists of members of the *Association Nationale pour la défense du territoire*. In less than a month groups had been formed in over 60 departments. By the end of March 40 deputies had either joined the Paris Association or had been instrumental in organising local groups. In Metz, 1,180 joined and it was claimed the national figure was 100,000. Many signatories were members of the National Guard. In Dijon, the Guard headquarters served as a recruiting centre for the Association. Sometimes the whole committee were guardsmen. The Association recalled the federations of 1815, both in its membership and its rhetoric.

Above all it was also a way to rally *mouvement* sympathisers, particularly officials, against the conservative trend of the new Périer government. Officials were at the heart of all the groups; every surviving membership list contains the name of the local mayor. In Dijon, seven municipal councillors, including the mayor, Hernoux, who was also the deputy, signed up [146].

THE CONSOLIDATION OF CONSERVATIVE ORLEANISM?

The ministry of 13 March, headed by Périer, was committed to *résistance* [*Doc. 32*]. Officials who refused to resign from the National Association found themselves out of their job, including Barrot and Lamarque. Périer was a tough Chief Minister, in control of both parliament and the king until his death from cholera in the spring of 1832. Press censorship was tightened and a law against large gatherings (*attroupements*) made it easier for the government to use force against crowds like that which had run amok on 14 February. Périer was proud to assert that the July revolution signified no more than a change of government, rejecting all *mouvement* demands for reform [*Doc. 32*]. Périer's hopes of containing criticism and popular unrest were to founder. The economic crisis was far from over; economic change continued to cause popular unrest. In 1832 France fell prey to the first outbreak of cholera.

7   POPULAR INSURRECTION AND THE REPUBLICANS

REPUBLICAN CLUBS

Before the 1830 revolution all left-wing critics tended to be lumped together. The revolution refined differences. The further 'left' a man's politics, the less likely he was to survive the Orleanist political game. *Aide-toi, le ciel t'aidera* was abandoned to the *mouvement* and began to demand the extension of the franchise. The most radical of the former liberals declared war on Périer. During the July Days republican clubs, the *Amis du Peuple*, and then the *Société des Droits de l'Homme*, were formed, ignoring the prohibitions of the Code. The *Amis* was the most prominent until the summer of 1832, when the *Droits de l'Homme* took over. Initially the *Amis* was conceived as a mass, public organisation. The membership of both societies overlapped and provincial groups might correspond with either. Local societies adopted a variety of names, often including 'patriotic' or 'national', or 'republican' in their titles. After October 1830 all clubs reverted to the standard formula of sub-dividing into cells of less than 20, usually organised in a hierarchy where only one member from each cell was known to members of other cells.

Both the *Amis* and the *Droits de l'Homme* were set up by radicals who had been in the *charbonnerie*, many of whom had become saint-simonians. Self-consciously imitating the Jacobin clubs of the 1790s, they asserted themselves as republicans and gradually became committed to radical social reform, though neither aspect was defined with any precision. One of the leaders was Godfrey Cavaignac, whose father was a prominent republican in the 1790s. Their sections often adopted names like Robespierre, Marat, Babeuf. Their guru in the immediate aftermath of the July Days was Buonarroti, Babeuf's ally in the Conspiracy of the Equals of 1796. This abortive attempt to seize power in the name of the 'people' and re-distribute property equally, led to Babeuf's execution and Buonarroti's imprisonment and subsequent career as an icon for clandestine insurrectionary groups throughout Europe. He eventually moved to Brussels, magnet to political exiles, where a number of the surviving Jacobins from the Convention had settled. In 1828 he published an account of the Equals' plans for a conspiracy in 1796, which became the 'little red book' of the younger generation of would-be revolutionaries. In an ideological sleight of hand, Buonarroti managed to merge an idealised Jacobin republicanism, typified by their 1793 constitution, which he re-printed in his book, with Babeuf's plans for social revolution, which would have shocked most Jacobins, who were respectful of property-rights. Immediately after the July Days Buonarroti secretly moved to Paris, where he lived under an assumed name to become the mentor of a new neo-Jacobin, Babouvist republicanism [*Doc. 33*].

At first the *Amis* ran public meetings and a poster campaign in which they criticised the absence of a referendum on constitutional revision and demanded the abolition of indirect taxes, although their pronouncements on the problems of the poor were often quite woolly [*Doc. 34*]. They had 150 members in October 1830 when the government successfully prosecuted them and banned their public meetings. Under the presidency of the radical doctor, Raspail, the *Amis* adopted a social programme. Each Parisian member was required to help educate the children of six poor families. In their leaflets and defence speeches during repeated prosecutions, republicans insisted that the main purpose of the clubs was to persuade others that France could adopt republican institutions without revolution and upheaval [*Doc. 35*]. But members were also ordered to provide themselves with weapons and take part in military training. The *Amis* were implicated in the riots which accompanied the trial of the ex-ministers, but were acquitted. Both societies joined in protests against indirect taxes. Orleanist governments routinely assumed that republicans were involved in any popular disorder.

Republican clubs were backed by some older-generation liberals, like Voyer d'Argenson, whose radicalism never dimmed and who became an enthusiastic patron of Buonarroti. Most of their leaders were men who had been students in the *charbonnerie* in the 1820s; Cavaignac, Blanqui, Buchez, Trélat and Raspail were temporarily united, although their ideas on means and goals were very varied. Some hoped to change society through parliament; indeed the Christian socialist, Buchez, was to write a 40-volume history of the assemblies of the 1789 Revolution. Blanqui was to spend his life dreaming of a Babouvist-style proletarian revolution – mostly in a prison cell.

Provincial groups depended on a combination of notables – or at least men who paid enough tax to vote: landowners, lawyers, doctors, editors of local papers. Their members included students, particularly of law, medicine and engineering, artisans and some peasants. Most members were in the National Guard and the clubs often attracted men, NCOs and other junior officers from the local regiment, some of them drawn, like Stendhal's young officer, Lucien Leuwen, by the boredom of military duties in a small provincial town. The republican club in Strasbourg in 1834 counted 30 officers from the local regiment among its 100 members.

Although the membership of these republican clubs was similar to the various radical groups of the 1820s, there were differences. The clubs made far more of an effort to recruit artisans; in 1834 the majority of members of the Parisian *Droits* were workers [134]. The most vigorous society, that of Arbois (Jura), was made up of wine producers, weavers, plasterers, carpenters and other workers [147].

THE REBELLION IN LYON, 1831

The deepening economic crisis, combined with the Orleanists' determination to hold to a *laissez-faire* strategy which they claimed was liberal, but which invariably protected property-owners, businessmen and merchants, meant that popular disturbances and artisan participation in clandestine clubs continued to increase. A high point was the insurrection of Lyon silkworkers in November 1831. Although the rebellion led to the forced evacuation of the prefect and the local garrison from Lyon for several days, the initial problem was economic. Lyon was dominated by the silk industry. It was an artisan industry, with small workshops in central and suburban Lyon (Croix Rousse), where purpose-built houses offered enough ceiling height to house the new Jacquard looms, but where rents were equally elevated. Previously autonomous master-weavers were forced to borrow to buy the new looms and turned to the merchants from whom, traditionally, they took their orders and sold their finished silk cloth. Merchants soon gained the upper hand and were able to dictate prices to the weavers. Simultaneously, during the Restoration, the silk industry lost many of its profitable foreign markets.

During the Restoration conflict between weavers and merchants intensified. Weavers, a large, literate and highly organised group, hoped that the new Orleanist regime would come to their help. In past centuries there had been a tradition of official arbitration in the fixing of a *tarif*. The practice had fallen into disuse long before 1789, but weavers continued to petition for its revival, hoping that the *conseil des prudhommes*, a committee on which weavers and merchants were represented, could be moulded for this function. In 1828, 80 weavers, increasing to 3,000 by 1834, grouped themselves into the Society of Surveillance and Mutual Indication. This was partly a mutual-aid insurance fund and partly a pressure group to demand a *tarif*. They set up a local newspaper to press their case [176]. In the autumn of 1831 they secured the ear of the prefect, Dumolard, and they believed that an official price agreement had been reached. The merchants thought otherwise. Paris disowned Dumolard's well-meant intervention, and in November 1831 weavers downed tools when merchants reneged on price agreements. Dumolard and the military commander were chased out of town by the Lyon National Guard, staffed by weavers, and the city remained in the hands of a revolutionary committee for ten days.

Although dramatic and deeply disturbing for the government, this rebellion posed no direct threat to the regime. The Lyon committee was a medley of weavers and radicals waiting for a chance to intervene in insurrection in Italy [48]. However, the despatch of extra troops to restore order under the command of marshal Soult, underlined the determination of the new regime to support 'employers' against 'workers' and thus helped to define social and political conflicts [*Doc. 36*].

MUTUAL-AID SOCIETIES

The key organisation in the campaign of the *canuts* (the local term used for a silkweaver) was the Mutualist Society. Mutual-aid societies were a nineteenth-century adaptation of traditional artisan craft organisations, *confraternités* and *compagnonnages*, which themselves often survived. In 1821 there were 128 mutual-aid societies in Paris with over 10,000 members. By 1840 there were 232 with more than 16,000 subscribers. A membership fee of between 10 and 30 francs was followed by monthly subscriptions of 1–2 francs, which provided sickness, old age, and occasionally unemployment benefit. Even the most modest societies paid out a death grant that paid for sociable funerals. Only the most prosperous artisans, nearly all male, could afford these fees and during the 1840s no more than 10 per cent of the working population of the capital was affiliated. The societies were practical evidence that workers could co-operate to reduce the uncertainties of life in a modern, increasingly market-directed economy. Officially they defied the *loi le Chapelier* of 1791, which banned workers' corporations, and article 291 of the Civil Code of 1804, which prohibited any association of more than 20 members. However, on the whole, successive governments between 1814 and 1848 left the mutual-aid groups alone, unless, like the Lyon society, they veered too close to politics. For instance, after the Lyon rebellion, government persecution of all societies caused the number of mutual-aid groups in Paris briefly to halve [174; 182].

STRATEGIES FOR OPPOSITION: NEWSPAPERS

The July Days had been provoked by the ban on the liberal press and the revised constitution claimed to reinstate press freedom. In consequence, there was an expansion in the number of papers printed in Paris and an unprecedented growth in politically orientated provincial papers, legitimist *Gazettes* and left-wing *Patriotes*. The left-wing papers were the focus for 50 or so local republican clubs. Cabet's *Populaire*, instantly gained subscribers from 70 assorted republican clubs and reading circles in 1833. The *Tribune des Départements* declared for a republic on 31 July and a handful of others began to heckle the conservative Orleanists, led by the *National*. Specific worker papers soon appeared in Paris, one of the longest-running being *L'Atelier*, started by Buchez. However, Lyon was the only provincial town with worker papers, and for a time it had two. In 1832–33 a small group of saint-simonian women ran an innovative enterprise, *La Femme libre*, written for working women like themselves. In 1834 the fourierist activist, Eugenie Niboyet, ran two short-lived women's papers in Lyon. Most newspapers were sold through annual subscriptions, still usually around 80 francs a year. The *Populaire*, which began as a Sunday paper, cost only 10 francs a year. Subscriptions soon topped 12,000. The paper was also sold on street corners, by hawkers. Monthly journals also offered good publicity. In the 1830s the fourierists relied on the *Phalanstère* to promote their ideas. In addition, newspapers would reprint a particular eye-catching story, most likely the most recent prosecution it had endured, in pamphlet-form. Tiny pamphlets were as popular with the republican clubs as they had been with *Aide-toi*. Their format was geared to their sales-staff and their audience. They were sold by *crieurs publics*, public hawkers. They were simple and cheap, directed at an artisan/peasant audience, summarising a recent radical event, or, typically, reproducing a 'Republican Catechism'. Charles Philipon ran a popular cartoon newspaper, *Le Charivari*. His most successful lithographer was Honoré Daumier, who immortalised Louis-Philippe as the (rotten) pear. As censorship tightened, Daumier showed the king, discarding his genial mask and costume of an ordinary citizen, to reveal himself as an authoritarian, militarist ogre [*Doc. 49.4*].

The response of the new Orleanist regime to the flowering of a critical newspaper press, part legitimist, but predominantly radical, was censorship. Legislation was gradually stiffened, with increasingly large sums demanded as caution money and more and more restrictions on content. Radical papers were frequently prosecuted. The *Tribune* was pursued in the courts 52 times in the first two years of the Orleanist monarchy. Jurors continued to acquit press 'offenders', but the cost of defending themselves undermined the solvency of papers, whose financial base was never secure.

The issue of press freedom became, as in the Restoration, a way of rallying opposition, although the alliance between radicals and legitimists was not renewed. A new association devoted to press freedom was set up under Cormenin, which changed its name in the summer of 1833 to *Association républicaine pour la défense de la liberté de la presse périodique et la liberté individuelle*. All the leading radicals contributed, including Cabet, Garnier-Pagès, Marrast, Cavaignac and Voyer d'Argenson and local groups were created. The association helped editors to prepare their defence and pay prosecution costs and fines. Members must have given generously. Its first task was to pay a 6,000-franc fine imposed on the *Tribune*.

STRATEGIES FOR OPPOSITION: BANQUETS AND FUNERALS

Given that large-scale public opposition was illegal, radical groups had to find alternative ways to show their strength without risking prosecution. Banquets and funerals were the most common. Throughout the constitutional monarchy prefects ground their teeth as opposition politicians toured the country calling for toast after toast reviling the government of the day, all on the basis of a modestly-priced subscription meal. Banquets were the most popular means of assembling large numbers to hear leading radical politicians. It was always galling to the government that local officials, particularly mayors, attended these events, even if their motives were, as they always claimed, simple curiosity. Funerals, always involving a large procession of mourners and lengthy speeches by the dead man's friends, provided an even better display of radical strength, because the procession took place along the street and there was thus no restriction on numbers, and no money to collect. The route could be planned to maximum radical advantage, tracking through effervescent artisan districts. The unpredictability of their timing was, however, a disadvantage for radicals who tried to plan their opposition events. Where you were buried was also a political statement. At his own request, Voyer d'Argenson was buried in the same grave as Buonarroti [147]. .

1832 was a busy year for deaths and riots. Cholera finally hit France in the early spring. Paris lost 18,000. In the peak month, April, 12,000 suffered a disgusting and terrifyingly rapid death. Cholera did not seek out the young, old and infirm, but proved equally adept at disposing of those in robust health. The cause of the disease was not known, but the detailed daily statistics, publicly displayed, revealed that artisan districts suffered disproportionately. The rumour developed among the poor that their water supply was being poisoned to keep them subdued. Bourgeois observers assumed that the poor succumbed to cholera more readily for moral reasons – they lived dissolute lives, were reluctant to work, refused to care for their families. Cholera was the AIDS epidemic of the time. It was not until the end of the century that developments in microscopes revealed that cholera was carried not by miasmas, foul smells, but was water-borne and working-class districts were likely to have worse water supplies than richer areas [108].

The wealthy did not escape. The Chief Minister, Périer, died, as did General Lamarque. On 5 June 1832, the funeral procession for Lamarque set off the most serious rioting since Lyon, imaginatively recollected in Hugo's *Les Misérables*. As the procession passed the Pont d'Austerlitz there was an attempt to seize the coffin and take it to the Panthéon, the former church of Saint-Geneviève in the Latin Quarter, which had been made into a secular shrine during the First Revolution and was restored to this status after the 1830 revolution. Barricades were erected in the same central artisan districts as in 1830. Artisan members of the *Amis du Peuple* were involved and they hoped that sympathetic politicians would take a lead. A few days earlier, on 28 May, 134 deputies had met at Laffitte's house, urged on by Odilon Barrot, and signed a declaration to renew their struggle to pursue the aims of 1789. However none of them, not even full-fledged republicans like Voyer d'Argenson, Garnier-Pagès and Cabet, would lead the rioting in the cloisters of the church of Saint-Merri or on the cluster of nearby barricades. The National Guard and troops were able to re-establish control on 6 June. The next day parliament declared a state of siege and trial by court martial for those arrested. Seven were sentenced to death, although the king commuted the sentences to deportation.

The refusal of radical leaders to support the rebellion encouraged the government. Official confidence was reinforced by the death of Napoleon's son, the duc de Reichstadt, in Vienna in July. Legitimist hopes disappeared in the embarrassing saga of the landing of the duchesse de Berri, widowed mother of the 'miracle child' Henri, in the legitimist heartland of Provence in May 1832. Her arrival in the formerly very loyal Vendée created such a minor display of enthusiasm that the duchesse fled. She was found to be pregnant yet again, in which condition, so long after her husband's assassination, even the most romantic legitimists found it difficult to sustain their loyalty. She was quietly deported.

THE SOCIAL QUESTION

In the 1830s the social question became the equivalent of 'green' issues in the late twentieth century. People of all shades of politics, from social catholics to republicans, via Orleanists, agonised over the problems of poverty and urbanisation. A socialist movement grew up with this as its central pre-occupation. Serialised novels by Victor Hugo and Eugène Sue appeared, plays attracted fascinated audiences, cartoons by Traviès, Jeanron and Charlet, and sometimes Daumier, idealised working people [56]. Serious statistical social surveys were made by Guépin, Villermé, Buret and others. Republican doctors like Raspail and Trélat ran free clinics for the poor. An *Association polytechnique* was set up by engineering students at the *école* after the July Days to run classes for workers. Orleanists, saint-simonians and republicans initially co-operated in the *Association pour l'instruction gratuite du peuple*. In early 1833 it was reborn as a republican organisation, with Cabet as secretary and Arago as vice-president. By the end of the year it had 3,000 subscribers, including 60 deputies. It ran 54 classes with 2,400 worker students. Lawyer and doctor subscribers offered their professional services free and a job-hunting facility was added. Similar philanthropic, educational and medical ventures were launched by saint-simonians and republicans in provincial France. An outstanding example was the work of Ange Guépin whose Industrial Society in Nantes ran evening classes and a free clinic for the poor, staffed by the doctor himself. He even secured a donation of 2,000 francs from the duc d'Orléans and 6,000 francs from the government for an apprenticeship scheme [148].

The social question was defined in the 1830s and novelists and newspaper editors made money exploiting it. Socialists contributed in practical ways to controlling unemployment, poor living conditions and encouraged literacy and better health. As yet, mainstream politicians were cautious in embracing the cause of the poor.

THE 'NEW WOMAN'

The legal status and social condition of women were much discussed during the July Monarchy, by both radicals and more conservative commentators. Observers claimed that changes in the structure of industry were eroding the family by obliging mothers and children to work. They noted that women workers were so badly paid that many were forced into prostitution [Docs 5 and 8]. In 1831, parliament considered the reintroduction of the right to divorce, abolished in 1814. There were demands for the revision of the Civil Code, which left women with fewer rights than children [Doc. 37]. There were a number of very visible women writers, notably the socialists George Sand and Flora Tristan, whose life-styles sparked moral outrage and a series of entertaining cartoons in the cartoon magazine, Charivari.

Pursuing their joint objectives of the liberation of workers and women, the saint-simonians, headed by their 'pope', Prosper Enfantin, tried to set up hostels for workers, to run evening classes and to recruit worker members. Female members like Desirée Gay and Eugénie Niboyet, some of them workers themselves, took a major part in this practical work. However, saint-simonian ideas on improving the status of women proved a great disappointment to their female members. Enfantin held rather Rousseauist ideas. He claimed that man and woman, as a couple, were the basis of society, but man provided the brains and woman the emotion. Although he asserted that their sect would not be complete until a female 'pope' had been found, he never found her. He eliminated women from senior posts in the movement. In November 1831, a substantial number of the most dynamic members broke with Enfantin because they thought his view of liberation was a deception. Many were also unhappy with his claim that female liberation should consist of sexual liberty as well as educational and professional opportunities [Doc. 37]. Like Fourier, Enfantin condemned monogamous marriage, and proposed 'experimental' marriage, or 'free unions' among sect members. In 1832, Enfantin, Michel Chevalier and other leaders were imprisoned for subverting morals. On their release a year later, the sect became increasingly eccentric. Some members set off on odysseys to find 'the woman' in Egypt, India and South America. Most drifted into fourierist socialism and/or into successful careers as government engineers [43; 51; 97; 120; 131; 149].

THE CAMPAIGN AGAINST THE REPUBLICANS

The republican clubs survived June 1832, although the *Amis du Peuple* was pursued with such vigour in the courts that members found it easier to re-group in the *Société des Droits de l'Homme*, which had until then taken a less prominent role. The *Droits* were far more systematic than the *Amis* in their recruitment. Membership increased substantially during 1833. As these were clandestine groups, no precise figures are available. In April, when Guizot urged parliament to ban all societies rigorously, he claimed that the *Droits* had 3,000 members. This seems to have been a serious under-estimation. The *Droits de l'Homme* recruited most successfully in eastern France; in early 1834 there were 60 cells in Dijon with about 1,000 members.

The increased size of republican clubs alarmed Orleanists because their growth coincided with industrial unrest as workers put pressure on employers to restore wage levels depressed during the economic crisis. The *Droits* was far less of an elite society than the radical groups of the 1820s. In Paris the majority of members were artisans, who often joined as workplace affiliations. Subscription rates were reduced to attract worker members. However republicans often only had a sketchy idea of artisan objectives. Their propaganda tended to talk about 'industrial freedom', whereas silk weavers and other arti-sans were often far more interested in the reintroduction of controls than their abolition. The republicans of Lyon were more pre-occupied with arguing the merits of Girondin and Jacobin republicanism than the problems of the *canuts*. Nonetheless, conservative Orleanists became convinced that republicans and artisans were becoming allies, especially in Lyon.

A three-pronged attack was launched against republicans: to muzzle their pamphlets, close their clubs and drive their newspapers into the ground. In February 1834, legislation was introduced to oblige *crieurs publics* (hawkers) to apply to the local prefect for a permit to trade, which could be revoked at any time. A draft bill was prepared which would bring all associations under strict prefectoral control, even those with fewer than 20 members. Artisans were con-cerned that this legislation would apply to craft associations and mutual-aid societies. On 14 February the Lyon silk weavers' societies brought all 25,000 looms in the city to a halt in protest against this proposal and to put pressure on merchants to agree to a set price for finished silk. This time the black banners calling *canuts* to 'Live work-ing or die fighting' were carried in vain. The societies lacked the cash to sustain a strike. Within a week weavers were back at work and the strike leaders were committed for trial [48].

With an appalling sense of timing, if workers were to be reassured that craft associations were not being targeted, the trial in Lyon of the strike leaders was scheduled to start on 9 April. The ban on associations became law on 10 April. The law, propelled through parliament by the Minister of Justice, Barthe, a former *carbonaro*, was passed by 246 votes to 154. No societies were exempted from prefectoral sanction and the members of an illegal association together with the owner of the property where it met would be subject to a 1,000-franc fine and a year's imprisonment.

The garrison in Lyon was increased in preparation for the trial; the government did not want to risk losing control again. The *palais de justice* was surrounded by armed men when the trial opened. When someone in the crowd started to throw stones at the soldiers, they opened fire. In the adjoining central districts where government buildings and weavers' quarters jostled one another between the arms of the two rivers, barricades were quickly manned by about 6,000 workers, many of them weavers. The artillery showed no mercy. By 15 April, 300 people were dead. The government insisted that this was a republican rebellion, but only 15 per cent of those arrested were members of either a political or an artisan association. Only 39 of the 100 men and women charged with conspiracy against the regime were actually republicans.

The response of Thiers, Minister of the Interior, to the events in Lyon in April 1834, was to order the arrest of up to 500 leading republicans in the Parisian *Droits de l'Homme* and to suspend publication of their main newspaper, the *Tribune*. Barricades were built in the central artisan quarters, traditional heart of revolt. The military response was rapid. A detachment marched into a house in the rue Transnonain, on the pretext that they had seen an armed man at one of the windows. A totally unarmed family, young and old, were killed. Daumier's evocative drawing of them all spread-eagled, at first glance merely sleeping, and then the eye takes in that the baby and the old man are dead, became one of the best-known condemnations of the Orleanist political and social attitudes [*Doc. 49.3*].

To justify the new repressive legislation and the brutal military strategy, Thiers put it about that for months the *Droits* had plotted a major conspiracy focused on Lyon to bring down the regime. It had long been the custom for members of the small cells of the secret societies of the era of the constitutional monarchy to visit other groups, carrying news and copies of leaflets and newspapers. Such visits redoubled in 1833 as the government's plans to crush the clubs became known. One of the most active of these agents in 1833–34 was Mascarène, a junior officer stationed in Lyon, who was also a government spy. Single-handed, and with the connivance of his commanding officer, he trawled the various clubs, with Mathieu, a genuine and long-established travelling salesman for republicanism. He convinced Mathieu that it was possible to use the clubs to bring down the regime. The rumours of a grand conspiracy were little more than the machinations of Mascarène, anxious to justify his agent's fee. It was a case of wish-fulfilment on both sides.

Having invented a virtual conspiracy, the government ordered the arrest in April 1834 of 2,000 would-be insurgents. Over a year later, 164 of them were finally brought to trial by the Chamber of Peers. In the meantime, the republican loner and adventurer, Fieschi, bungled his attempt to assassinate the king in July 1835, killing 18 and wounding 22 bystanders. The event destroyed all sympathy for the detainees. They were finally sentenced in January 1836. Leading republicans like Cavaignac and Cabet had fled to England. The rest received a range of sentences, except Mascarène, who was acquitted. The trial took almost as long as the terms ultimately served. The detainees were pardoned in 1837 and the exiles allowed to return in 1840 [147].

The Orleanist approach to political opposition was curious; comprehensive repressive legislation was accompanied by brutal military action. The lengthy inquisitorial process was simply standard judicial process, nearly always revealing the gullibility of both sides. Resulting prison sentences were far more modest than those accorded by the successor to the Orleanists, Napoleon III. Prisoners rarely served more than a year, amnesties being the standard form to accompany a royal wedding or birth (and Louis-Philippe was the father of a large family). The philosophy of trial and punishment for political crimes may have been related to a determination to avoid the excesses (and bad publicity) of the Terror of the early 1790s. It could not have been that people believed that insurgents were 'cured' of their awkward attitudes by a short, sharp shock, because political prisoners were in constant contact with each other while in jail, reinforcing their sense of grievance.

If the actual punishment of republicans was mild, the nascent republican movement was fairly comprehensively squashed by the new law against associations and the pursuit of radical newspapers in the courts. The *Tribune* folded in May 1835, the victim of 111 prosecutions and 20 convictions, adding up to 49 years in jail for the editor.

Fieschi's attempt on the king's life provided the excuse to try to eliminate the radical press entirely. The September Press Laws of 1835 raised caution money and sentences yet again, withdrew press offences from the scrutiny of juries, denied newspapers the opportunity to publish details of a trial, and finally banned any reference to republicanism in the press. Even cartoonists like Daumier had to turn to social criticism.

Despite censorship, the press prospered. Daumier's social caricatures, particularly of the renowned theatrical swindler character, Robert Macaire, side-stepped censorship [155]. Major national papers, such as the *Le Populaire, L'Atelier, Le National,* and later *La Réforme* were all sharply critical of Orleanist policies. The only real casualties were the radical local papers, which were always undercapitalised and could not have survived the competition of the new cheaper national papers, *La Presse* and *Le Siècle,* which by 1846 sold 22,000 and 33,000 copies respectively. Emile de Girardin's *La Presse* was launched in 1836 at half the normal price and sustained itself by out-selling its rivals. One of Girardin's most successful ploys was the serialised novel. *Le Siècle* was started the same year by Armand Dutacq. Both eschewed high politics and appealed to a broader, less wealthy audience than most existing papers. Technical developments which improved the quality and reduced the price of lithographic reproduction facilitated the publication of newspapers devoted to caricature, particularly Philipon's short-lived *La Caricature,* and more successful, *Le Charivari.* Mass journalism took a step further in 1843 with *L'Illustration,* although at 36 francs annual subscription this illustrated weekly sold to a well-heeled clientele. Traditional papers had to adopt the serialised novel. In 1842, the *Journal des Débats* secured Eugène Sue's *Les Mystères de Paris* and readers queued for their copies.

In reality the Orleanist regime had little to fear from criticism. The 'republican' threat was largely of its own imagining. Republicans had no precise political or social programme. Only a tiny minority countenanced insurrection as the way forward; this was very apparent in 1832 and in 1834. It was made embarrassingly plain in May 1839 when a thoroughly recidivist insurgent, Blanqui, tried to scrape together a Babouvist revolution, inspired by the ideas of Buonarroti. Blanqui managed to run successive small secret societies, the *Family* and later, *Seasons,* despite the 1834 legislation, drawing on the traditional artisan clientele of the cafés of the worker quarters of central Paris. These were dedicated insurrectionary groups, focused on weapons and ammunition, not books, literacy and free clinics. Blanqui hoped that May 1839 would be propitious for a rising of 'the people', even though the nucleus of his group were disaffected bourgeois intellectuals like himself. France was experiencing minor economic setbacks, she was 'between' governments, it was a race-day holiday and troops and National Guardsmen were likely to be at the races.

In the event Blanqui's carefully constructed plan to seize strategic central buildings, such as the Hôtel-de-Ville and the nearby prefecture of police and Palais de Justice, totally misfired [*Doc. 38*]. Troops and National Guardsmen turned out against his small worker contingents. A revolt planned to start at 2.30pm was over by 11pm; 66 rebels were killed, including five women, always a visible force on barricades. Blanqui, Barbès and 700 companions (almost the total complement of the insurgents) were rapidly rounded up. The bulk of those arrested were the same sort of skilled artisans, workers in textiles, metal workers, cabinet-makers and men in the building trades, who had fought in July 1830. In June 1839, 22 of the leaders were tried by the Chamber of Peers. Attempts were made to link them with Fieschi and to claim that Meunier, who had tried to kill the king in December 1836, was a member of the *Families*. Blanqui and his allies were incarcerated in the remote fortress of Mont St Michel for the rest of the reign. This time no opportune anniversary was allowed to offer the chance of an amnesty [147].

If republicans offered no real alternative to the Orleanists, Louis-Philippe made serious efforts to enlist Bonapartist sentiments behind his throne. Many republicans continued to nourish fond memories of the Emperor. The Bonapartism of the 1830s seems to have been a compound of nostalgia for military glory, recalled in novels, plays, songs and paintings, and the conviction that Napoleon had been a vital component in the revolutionary process, saving the republic in 1799 and facilitating the completion of legislation which created the modern French state. Louis-Philippe was aware of the publicity potential of harnessing Bonapartism to Orleanism [49]. Monuments erected or modified by the Orleanists celebrated Napoleon as the soldier of the Revolution. The July Column honoured the dead of the 1830 revolution, who were re-buried in its foundation, along with the memory of the Empire. In 1836, Thiers instituted the construction of the Arc de Triomphe which Napoleon had planned [33; 121; 197]. Louis-Philippe ordered and supervised a complete restoration of the palace of Versailles, the centre-piece of which were galleries which displayed the history of France, focusing on the Revolution. The climax was a series of massive paintings eulogising Napoleon's military victories, mostly executed, in prosaic style, by the king's favourite painter, Vernet [56; 120].

In 1840, apparently as a consequence of numerous petitions received by the government since 1830, Thiers announced the official, and very theatrical, return of Napoleon's ashes to France and deposition in Les Invalides [50]. The king hoped thereby that Imperial glory would rub off on him. Instead, Louis-Philippe was caricatured as a pathetic imitation Bonaparte, on a broken-down nag dragging himself around a depressed and dejected countryside [*Doc. 49.5*]. Credit for the Bonapartist revival went to the nephew, Louis-Napoleon, who wrote *Napoleonic Ideas* [*Doc. 39*], in which he embroidered the mythology presented in Napoleon's memoirs, that his great-uncle had been a constitutional liberal at heart. He followed this with two attempts to gain the support of local garrisons for a seizure of power, first in Strasbourg in 1836, and then in Boulogne in 1840. Both were damp squibs; the nephew was swiftly shipped off to America in 1836 and in 1840 confined to comfortable imprisonment in the fortress of Ham in Picardy. This time there was no question of an early release and Louis-Napoleon attracted only a very limited group of devotees in France. The Bonapartist legend was a different matter. In 1845 the first volume of Thiers's history of the Consulate and Empire appeared.

By 1840 Orleanism had survived sustained popular unrest and republican, socialist and Bonapartist opposition. What was the recipe for its survival? Economic prosperity and the inability of its enemies to offer united activity seem the most likely explanation, together with the determination of Orleanist politicians to avoid confrontation and conflict in parliament.

8 LIBERTY AND ORDER: A *JUSTE MILIEU* SECURED?

The motto of the July Monarchy was 'Liberty and Order'. The electoral and educational systems combined to restrict liberty to those with *capacité*. Order meant using the judicial system, censorship and the army to maintain this narrow elite. The maintenance of public order was always the prime requisite for politicians who never forgot that their power was based on insurrection. The regime was often bleakly referred to by the month of its invention, the 'July' Monarchy. The Orleanists claimed to represent, not an ideology, but a 'middle way', a predictable paranoia after years of revolution [40].

The king cultivated popularity and was aware of the need to make himself visible and available. In the early years he repeatedly toured the country with his large family in tow and there was some enthusiasm for this 'people's' king. At first his court was very open, the elaborate uniforms and traditional court dress of the Restoration were abandoned, apparently creating some problems sifting doormen from ministers [119]. Formal ceremonial was gradually restored. Can a ruler's popularity be gauged by how many assassination attempts he survived? That the six failed presumably tells us no more about mass hostility than the effusive multi-signature letters of congratulation he received on each occasion tell us about the value placed on him. It was his heir, the distinctly radical duc d'Orléans, who died first, in a carriage accident in 1842, leaving the duc de Nemours, more in keeping with conservative Orleanism, to succeed. Louis-Philippe's numerous official portraits document his attempt to transform his image from citizen king to an almost-Bourbon. A flattering equestrian portrait of the king and his sons, painted in 1840, shows them galloping through the main gate of Versailles, emblazoned with fleurs de lys and other Bourbon emblems [155]. Daumier preferred to draw him as a fat Napoleonic wanna-be, on a broken-down nag [*Doc. 49.5*]. If Lamartine is to be believed, Louis-Philippe bored rather than annoyed people. He was inclined to give long speeches and his moral family life left little room for gossip.

ORLEANIST POLITICAL LIBERTY

There were 15 coalitions between 1830 and 1840 and a single government from October 1840 until the February revolution in 1848. This did not mean that the political scene was wracked with uncertainty up to 1840 and blessed with sublime security subsequently. All the Orleanist governments merely involved shuffling the same pack of names. There was never a dominant party of government, nor a resolute one in opposition. Radical critics became known as *gauche dynastique*, *tiers parti*, the most extreme republicans, socialists – or both. On the right were a small group of legitimists, no more united than any other formation. Groups still tended to coalesce around individuals who were perceived to have influence and patronage. In the 1831 elections, the *'mouvement'* had done quite well, but those of 1834 resulted in 320 men prepared to support the government and only 90 left-wing critics. The left never recovered its initial appeal and the elections of 1837, 1839, 1842 and 1846 saw the Chamber more and more fragmented. Guizot could only count 23 close supporters when he became Minister of Foreign Affairs and a senior partner in the government of October 1840. Indeed, successive governments tended to be identified by the date of their inception, because none of them corresponded to a precise set of political principles, or even objectives. Few topics stimulated real division in parliament, whether foreign affairs, railway construction, social legislation or proposals for suffrage reform [59].

MORAL ORDER

To set the moral tone of the new regime, in 1832 Guizot revived the *Académie des Sciences Morales et Politiques* which Napoleon had dissolved in 1803 because it was too critical of his government. Members included Guizot himself, Victor Cousin, Alexis de Tocqueville and the historian Michelet, both critical of conservative Orleanism, as well as Dr Villermé [*Doc. 5*] and Buret [*Doc. 6*]. Their reports on the working and living conditions of the poor were commissioned by the Academy, who gave Buret a prize for his statistical comparison of France and England. Both reports stimulated much critical comment of Orleanist social policies. An outstanding academician was Adolphe Blanqui. He was the most famous liberal economist of the day and, like Villermé, a man with a keen conscience, eager to see a positive solution to poverty and nervous of leaving the development of society entirely to chance. Blanqui, who succeeded to the Chair of his tutor, the liberal economist J.-B. Say at the Conservatoire, who wrote the standard history of the European economy, never lost his concern that the elites should address the huge and growing disparity of wealth, but remained a proponent of *laissez-faire*. He was a co-founder of the *Journal des Economistes* in 1841, a periodical founded with the twin aims of analysing the most efficacious route to economic growth and combating socialist solutions to poverty. He argued, ineffectively but vigorously, that protectionist tariffs were counter-productive in a liberal system.

The role of the liberal state was constantly rehearsed. After much debate, legislation restricting child labour in 1841 set the minimum age for employment at eight years, but it only applied to businesses with more than ten workers and relied on self-regulation [89]. Orleanists were alarmed by the correlation between economic crises and popular unrest and the propaganda of socialists, but they held to the philosophy of Say and Sismondi, the renowned liberal economists of the day, that the economy should be self-balancing. How did Orleanists square this with active state intervention, and in more positive directions than mere strike breaking? The long-established tradition of large-scale public works was expanded. Increased sums were invested in improving canal and river navigation (1835), extending the power of communes to expand road-building programmes through taxation (1836), improving Le Havre and other ports (1839), even before the issue of a rail network was addressed [151].

Church and state struggled to tolerate each other in their common pursuit of moral social order. Pope Gregory XVI persuaded the clergy to say prayers for the July Days and the new king, whatever their private thoughts about the Bourbons, and we have seen that the Périer government squashed popular anti-clerical demonstrations. But the government refused to repair the residence of the Archbishop of Paris after 14 February 1831 and the church of Sainte-Geneviève was restored as the secular shrine, the Panthéon. Salaries paid to bishops were halved. The Church had its own problems. The newspaper, *L'Avenir*, run by the abbé Lammenais, Lacordaire, a priest, and the comte de Montalembert, challenged the authority of the state over religion and demanded that the Church appeal to the masses with a radical, democratic message. When Gregory XVI refused, Lammenais eventually broke with the Papacy. Social catholics demanded that the Church recognise its responsibilities to the poor. In 1833 the social catholic, Ozanam, founded the Society of Saint-Vincent-de-Paul and by 1847 it was handing out a million francs in charity each year. Religious orders like the Benedictines and the Dominicans were allowed to return. Lacordaire transfixed congregations of 10,000 at Notre-Dame. The Church was gradually beginning to realise that it had to popularise its appeal. The cult of the Sacred Heart, increased emphasis on the role of Mary, and a reluctant positive response to the new wave of visions and consequent pilgrimages reduced the dominance of fire and brimstone in popular religion [64; 75; 84; 107]. In 1839, the intransigent ultra, de Quélen, died and a bourgeois prelate, Monseigneur Affre, was appointed Archbishop of Paris. The Soult–Guizot governing coalition, formed in 1840, tried to exploit his moderation to persuade legitimists to draw closer to the regime [59].

Although bridges between Church and state were built, many foundered when it came to education. Like all contemporaries, Orleanists were convinced of the fundamental role of education for all. Not the same education: the new primary schools educated the masses, the rich monopolised the *lycées* and higher education. The Guizot law of 1833 gave the Minister of Education (now firmly separated from religion) the power to oblige all communes to run primary schools for boys, appointing a lay teacher, or in conjunction with the Church. Each department was to found an *école normale*, a training college for teachers (male). Boys of poor parents were to receive free education, others paid a fee. By 1840, only 6,000 of the 37,000 communes had no school. Although a quarter of boys, and even more girls, never went to school, by 1848, 3.25 million children attended primary schools. The legislation had a rapid impact on basic literacy. In 1829, 45 per cent of army conscripts could read. By 1848 the figure was 64 per cent [73; 76].

Nearly half of all the 60,000 secondary pupils and large numbers of primary ones attended Church schools. The new Assumptionists, the Marists and the Jesuits ran schools for the legitimist notables. An anti-Jesuit scare was started in 1843 by leading Sorbonne academics, Quinet and Michelet. Although they were dismissed, their criticism stirred up yet another attempt to expel the Jesuits [62]. In the name of 'freedom of education', promised in the Charter, Montalembert ran a campaign in the Chamber of Peers against the right of the state-run University to monitor church secondary schools. Many of these were not of the elite variety, but 'little seminaries' educating boys from humble backgrounds, ostensibly exclusively for the priesthood. In the mid-1840s, Louis Veuilliot regularly sold 6,000 copies of *L'Univers*, a catholic paper devoted to condemning Orleanist Voltaireanism as godless and therefore immoral [59]. The uneasy relationship between Church and state ensured that the Orleanist regime never succeeded in asserting its moral role.

A COMMUNICATIONS REVOLUTION

The July Monarchy witnessed a comprehensive revolution in a variety of forms of communication which served the cause of Orleanist 'Order'. Royal roads were improved; 53 were in good order at the beginning of the reign, 96 at its end. The development of local roads was even more dramatic. In 1830 none were reliable, in 1848 36,000 miles were usable all year round. These changes promoted a market economy, but the cost and speed of road transport still presented limitations. At the end of the reign the journey from Paris to Strasbourg took 49 hours and a passenger fare of 0.14 francs a kilometre eliminated all but the rich. The big difference came with railways. From 1837 discussions opened to add railways to the brief of the public works portfolio when it became apparent that private finance was inadequate. The first trains travelled at 30 miles per hour, five times the speed of coaches and Lyon and Strasbourg were only ten hours away at a fare of 0.06 francs per kilometre (third class) and 0.10 first class. Railway building got under way in 1842 and by 1870 Paris was linked to every French city by rail. By 1860 every major city was within 16 hours' journey from Paris.

The first railways brought the railway postal cars where mail was sorted on the train. They also carried newspapers. Railways centralised France in other ways. Railway finance was provided by the big Paris banking houses like Rothschilds and Laffitte. The Railway laws, starting in 1842, gave the central government massive power to expropriate property, fix fares and enforce standards. From 1840 the metric system was no longer optional. The first electric telegraph line linked Paris and Rouen, faster and more reliably than earlier semaphore aerial telegraphs which required stations every seven miles and were immobilised in bad weather. By 1851 Paris was thus connected with every departmental capital [151].

The Orleanists never forgot that their power depended, not on parliamentary majorities, but on the military, and this meant the army, because the National Guard, despite the interminable portraits made of Louis-Philippe in its uniform, proved as unwilling to suppress popular unrest as they had during the Restoration. Improved roads, and even more, the railways, were an important ally. By 1848 a battalion could be moved 125 miles in seven hours, whereas before the railways it would have taken seven hours to march 17 miles. In 1840 Thiers ordered the construction of a ring of forts around Paris, where troops could be in readiness, both to control popular insurrection from within and to defend the city against a foreign aggressor [141]. Unfortunately for the Orleanists, neither the rail network, nor the forts, were completed by 1848.

9 HOW WAS IT THAT THE ORLEANIST MONARCHY WAS ELIMINATED IN A REVOLUTION?

Very few contemporaries expected revolution in 1848. Most historians, with the exception of Marx, for whom February was yet another 'bourgeois' revolution, refer to a 'coincidence of crises', political and economic. Yet the foreign, social and electoral strategies of the Orleanist regime met a sustained barrage of criticism, laced with the titillation of a succession of scandals affecting public figures.

One of the most frequently-rehearsed themes of criticism in parliament was foreign policy. Government critics bemoaned the loss of Empire and in 1840, when Napoleon's ashes were in transit to Les Invalides, encouraged the government to have a little war with Britain. Conservative Orleanists steered a cautious strategy of survival, conscious that France's former enemies remained suspicious that Imperial ambitions might be revived. Guizot promoted an entente cordiale with Britain, which tended to grow more or less harmonious depending on whether the anti-French Palmerston was in charge in London. *Rapprochement* with Britain was forced on France, partly because it needed British investment in railways, and partly because the alternative was international isolation by the other major states, all of which remained absolute monarchies. Reciprocal state visits were exchanged in the 1840s between London and Paris. Minor incidents could balloon into major crises. There was endless debate in the 1840s over which prince, of which royal house, should marry which Spanish princess. Colonial issues could create quite a storm. The French conquest of Algeria proceeded unchecked, but when France annexed Tahiti in 1844 and expelled the English missionary and consul, Pritchard, Guizot was forced to offer Pritchard compensation. Although he never paid, radical critics in the Chamber of Deputies exploded in wrath at the slight to French patriotism [59; 192].

The lack of idealism among Orleanists was criticised by diverse critics, from Alexis de Tocqueville, who thought they should show concern for contemporary social problems, and Karl Marx, who dismissed them as self-interested fat cats [*Doc. 40*]. Commentators observed the growing social problems and divisions. Orleanist governments were accused of being committed to retaining power for a tiny elite and disregarding contemporary poverty. Both at the time and since they have received a bad press compared with the utopian ideals of reformers.

SOCIALIST CRITICISM OF ORLEANISM

During the 1830s Orleanist socio-economic attitudes were attacked from all sides. Social catholics, like the legitimist deputy, Villeneuve-Bargemont, a former Restoration prefect, urged the re-birth of private charity and moral altruism, which he contrasted with contemporary neglect of the poor [114]. The Orleanist ruling elite was typically categorised by contemporary social critics, novelists and cartoonists like Daumier, Travies and Charlet, for its bourgeois self-satisfaction [80; 110]. Radicals and socialists were preoccupied with the perceived polarisation of society into warring classes. The term socialist was used in the 1830s and 1840s to describe a range of solutions to the much publicised 'social question', some utopian, some reformist, some state-directed, some autonomous. Almost none were revolutionary. Indeed, recognising that the social problem lay in social antagonisms, variously described, but basically between haves and have-nots, socialists offered ways to reduce conflict. All shared the same conviction as the social catholics, and indeed the Orleanists themselves, that the social question was a moral, not an economic issue. The difference between them was that socialists proffered economic solutions.

Socialists were optimistic that solutions to the problems of poverty and decreasing worker independence could be reached through education and the Almighty [45; 54]. All perceived the problem as one of nascent capitalism, relentless competition, between workers for jobs, and between employers for sales. All were convinced that the solution lay in eliminating the confrontation and competition that seemed inherent in an emerging market economy. They were unanimous in believing that the answer lay in some form of association, which would give workers the economic security they had lost. These schemes ranged from adaptations of traditional artisan confraternities, or the newer mutual-aid societies, to utopian plans for a new world. They were all convinced that a perfect society could be secured. Their notions brought them into direct conflict with Orleanist economic liberalism [66; 147].

One of the most active groups were fourierists, many of them former saint-simonians, led by Victor Considérant, an engineer with an enthusiasm for Fourier. Fundamentally a middle-class movement of do-gooders outside Paris, the fourierists first tried to create an autonomous *phalange*, then settled for a 'right to work', underwritten by state intervention, as the solution to poverty [181]. Etienne Cabet was a utopian, but unlike Fourier, whose *phalange* would have been a profit-sharing commune in which private ownership and social inequality would have survived, Cabet's Icarie would have established total equality. Its members would have agreed to pool all their property and share absolutely everything equally, living in identical homes, receiving the same food from communal warehouses, enjoying a money-free society. Cabet published his *Voyage en Icarie*, in which he described his perfect society, in 1841. It had gone through five editions by 1848. His Icarian movement, consisting of up to 100,000 associates, nearly all of whom were traditional craftsmen, was the first – and only – mass artisan formation of the day. Cabet was inclined to call himself a communist, because he argued for communal property [99].

In the 1830s, communism was used more frequently to describe the ideas of those, like Auguste Blanqui, who followed Buonarroti and hoped to establish an egalitarian society, not through agreement, but revolution. Blanqui was one of very few early socialists who believed that revolution was the way to secure social change [45]. Others looked for more piecemeal, gradual change rooted in traditional artisan organisations. Such worker co-operatives took a variety of forms. Buchez set up a jewellers' co-operative in Paris in the early 1830s which survived for half a century. It was never very prosperous and its total membership never exceeded 18. Autonomous producer co-operatives were tried in various trades, from baking to textiles. Some were self-financing, like that of Buchez, others relied on middle-class patronage to get started. In newspaper articles, published in 1841 as *The Organisation of Work*, Louis Blanc took up the idea, which the fourierists had already floated, of the organisation of work [112]. He argued that the state should be the 'banker to the poor' [*Doc. 41*]. The government should lend money to groups of workers to set up social workshops. After a year the loan would be repaid and the workshop run its own affairs, the state merely overseeing it at a distance. Cut-throat competition, which he described in detail, using the evidence of Villermé and Guépin, would thus wither.

Other socialists thought the best form of association was a union of workers, combining together to secure improvements in wages and conditions. In the early 1840s Flora Tristan tried to mobilise workers into an Owenite mass union, which, she argued, with an annual subscription of two francs per head, would have the resources to finance a spokesman in parliament. Proudhon, famous for his 'What is Property?', published in 1841 [*Doc. 41*], wanted a Peoples' Bank to be set up, which would be a clearing house for investment, raw materials, tools and finished goods, organised in an elaborate form of barter [68; 147; 195].

Most of these socialist writers were middle-class and most of the investment for experimental workshops came from philanthropic doctors, lawyers, businessmen or landowners, who had been saintsimonians and often moved on to fourierism. State engineers, graduates of the *école polytechnique*, were a formative influence. This socialism was expressed in newspapers, pamphlets and books, and in practical schemes. Socialism was rooted in artisan grievances and the projects were often shaped around traditional artisan organisations. Artisan socialists were the sort of people who had been in the *charbonnerie* and the *Droits de l'Homme*; craft workers in the textile trades, tailors, weavers; building workers; skilled operatives in the various luxury trades of the capital – metallurgical, shoe-makers, hatters, etc. Early socialism had its artisan writers, such Perdiguier, Nadaud, Deroin, and its poets [66]. Indeed, worker poets became a cult for middle-class socialists during the 1840s [137]. There were thriving artisan-owned and run newspapers. Cabet started *Le Populaire*, revived on his return from exile in 1840, but it was owned, run and partly written by artisans. If *Icarie* was a dream world, *Le Populaire* made detailed statistical analyses of wage levels and workers' problems, reported to them by their readers. Buchez started *L'Atelier*, an artisan-run and owned newspaper which backed his brand of Christian socialism and campaigned against women workers. Socialist theorists were as slow as republicans to connect with the less advertised but far more ubiquitous rural poverty.

The publication, in 1840–41, of three influential and popular socialist works by Blanc, Proudhon and Cabet, indicates substantial criticism of Orleanism. However, aside from Blanqui and a handful of associates, none of the early socialists wanted to overthrow the established regime. Cabet's Icarians represented varied and specific problems in their trades. The movement had no formal structure nor did it have any direct impact on politics. Indeed, from 1846 the movement fell apart and *Le Populaire* lost a third of its subscribers. By 1848 the most active socialist groups were the fourierists and effectively their plans for the organisation of work were close to the expanding public works programme of the regime itself. Fourierists enthusiastically worked with Orleanist royals and notables in Mettray, a reform colony, in which young offenders were taken away from prison, taught a trade and given a basic education. It is true that socialists like Cabet, Proudhon, Considérant and especially Blanc, took a leading role in the early months of the Second Republic, but there was no sign that they were about to change the world before the February revolution [147].

POLITICAL CORRUPTION

If there were voices raised about Orleanist neglect of the poor, there were also complaints of corruption within the elite. In 1847, during a criminal trial involving a mining company, it was claimed that one of their associates, General Cubières, a member of the Chamber of Peers and former minister, had bribed a fellow peer, Teste, then Minister of Public Works. In July, both were fined and deprived of civil rights. Teste, who had attempted to kill himself, was also jailed for three years. In August, another peer, the duc de Choiseul-Praslin, was accused of murdering his wife. He actually committed suicide in jail. A rash of such cases came to light [59; 91; 151]. Balzac delighted his readers with imaginary reconstructions of similar scandals in *Le Cousin Pons* and Eugène Sue and Alexandre Dumas followed suit [*Doc. 43*].

THE BANQUET CAMPAIGNS

The February revolution was the consequence of confrontation following the government's ban on a reform banquet. Were the banqueteers the architects of revolt? What part did the banquets play in bringing about the revolution? Banquets were a recognised and long-established method of rallying people to a political cause, as we have already seen. When the extension of voting rights for parliamentary elections was debated in March 1831, *Aide-toi* produced pamphlets promoting the case for a wider electorate and for more than a year organised banquets to fête radical deputies. In 1833 and 1834 the *Droits de l'Homme* demanded a democratic electorate, variously asking for the vote for all National Guardsmen, or all taxpayers.

After the Reform Bill was passed in England in 1832, the Chartists campaigned for universal male suffrage. Following the modest extension of the right to vote in 1831, some French radicals began rather tentatively to make similar demands. Radicals on both sides of the

Channel were in contact. Blanc spent his exile (1834–40) in London and was influenced by his English colleagues. Buonarroti's popular account of the 1796 conspiracy was translated by Bronterre O'Brien, editor of the *Poor Man's Guardian*. In 1840, *Le National* and 30 local papers combined with moderate left-wing deputies like Laffitte, Arago and Dupont de l'Eure to organise petitions demanding the vote for all National Guardsmen. Since anyone who could afford a weapon and uniform could be a guardsman, this was a distinctly radical proposal. Their petitions secured a record 188,000 signatures, but Arago alarmed parliament when he compared their campaign with the work of the Convention in 1793–94. He observed that suffrage reform ought to be linked with social reform to help those out of work in the current economic crisis, if workers were to be kept from becoming enemies of the regime. Thiers brushed the reform plan aside with an argument agreeable to the elite, that there was no reason for national sovereignty to be translated into votes for all.

When the reform petition was passed over in parliament in 1840, the organisers appealed to the country. Nearly 100 reform committees were set up in the departments, with enthusiastic support in eastern France and Normandy, but less interest in Brittany and the southwest. A vigorous banquet campaign was held during the summer, with dinner at four francs a head. Banquets were held in Paris, including a communist one in Belleville. The government banned a banquet planned for the artisan district of Saint-Antoine timed to commemorate 14 July and the ceremony transferring the remains of those who died in the 1830 revolution below the new *colonne de juillet* at the Bastille. The banquets addressed other issues, including patriotic criticism of the government's unwillingness to go to war with Britain. The campaign fizzled out in mid-October 1840 when Darmès joined the ranks of would-be royal assassins, encouraged, it was claimed, by the reformers [41].

Electoral reform was resurrected annually, and was always greeted by Guizot with sympathetic understanding, but was consistently resolutely deferred, on the grounds that the existing system was still new and that 200-franc voters could represent everyone. Reformers were no nearer to a consensus on a common strategy. Barrot and Thiers's *gauche dynastique* only wanted to tinker with the franchise, whereas Garnier-Pagès, along with Marrast, editor of *Le National,* hoped for universal male suffrage. In 1841, Ledru-Rollin, a republican lawyer who spoke for the defendants in the 1835 conspiracy trial, took Garnier-Pagès's parliamentary seat when he died. From 1843 Ledru-Rollin's new newspaper, *La Réforme,* edited by Godefroy Cavaignac and the socialist, Louis Blanc, demanded universal suffrage as part of a programme of radical social reform, including state loans to artisan social workshops.

It was not only radicals for whom electoral reform encompassed more than the size of the electorate. Reformers like Duvergier de Hauranne argued for a redistribution of constituency boundaries, to correspond to economic change [*Doc. 44*]. Population movements and economic development left the rural south over-represented and the industrial north under-represented. The argument was just, the potential consequences political dynamite. The rural areas elected government men, the towns, radicals. Left-wing candidates secured majorities in cities like Paris, Lille, Marseille, Nantes and Bordeaux. In 1842, 12 of the 14 deputies for the Seine were left-wingers. In 1840, the Guizot government had a precarious hold on power. Exploiting patronage to the full, 40 per cent of MPs were place-men, in the pay of the government. The election of 1842 gave Guizot a potential majority of 60, although sometimes it fell to eight. In 1846 his majority rose; his allies numbered 291, his opponents 168. At the height of his parliamentary strength, Guizot had no need to consider parliamentary reform [101].

Reformers criticised the dominance of a narrow group of notables in politics. Some proposed that deputies should receive a salary and that the 500-franc tax qualification for deputies should be abolished. The total of potential candidates was no more than 50,000. The largest category were landowners. In the 1840s, a candidate would need an income of at least 2,500 francs to qualify; a *lycée* teacher earned about 1,500 francs. Left-wing deputies tended to be nearer the 500-franc minimum, which would indicate that they would gain with these reforms, but some of the richest were also the most radical, including Hartmann, an Alsatian cotton magnate with an 8,000-franc tax bill and a salon in Paris.

In 1847, Duvergier de Hauranne, a moderate reformer, introduced a proposal that 100-franc taxpayers should be enfranchised. It was defeated by 252 votes to 154. Charles Rémusat's more modest suggestion that membership of parliament should be made incompatible with certain official appointments was defeated more narrowly. Reformers decided to repeat the strategy of 1840 and take the case to the country. Circumstances were very different.

ECONOMIC CRISIS, 1845–48

Since 1845 France had been experiencing a severe economic crisis. An unrealistic boom in railway shares in the early 1840s was followed by a sudden loss of confidence and the collapse in share prices, which spread through other companies in panic selling at the Paris Bourse. Commercial and industrial activity were affected and wage cuts, underemployment and unemployment followed, with consequent social unrest. As in the early 1830s, things were made much worse by the potato blight and harvest failures of 1845, 1846 and 1847. Food prices rocketed, causing grain and bread riots. The usual complaints about government policies, particularly against indirect taxes and the erosion of communal rights ensued.

Cities suffered most acutely, especially Paris, the heart of the luxury trades. Traditional craft industries producing high-quality luxury goods suffered as always in a crisis. Since the 1830s the working population of the capital had diversified with railway workers at Batignolles and the *gare* d'Orléans and an increased number of migrant building workers. In addition, factories were emerging in the outlying suburbs of La Villette, Aubervilliers, Pantin, Belleville and Charonne. New districts were being carved out in the fields between the old *octroi*, the boundary within which indirect taxes were paid, and the line of forts started under Thiers's orders in 1840. Unemployment in these industries and in all French cities was tackled by the usual mix of private and municipal charity. Charity workshops were started. No one counted the potential claimants, hoping that the crisis was a temporary blip. By February 1848 it was in its third year with no sign of abatement. It was reckoned that there were about 10,000 out of work in the capital [126; 147; 183].

THE BANQUET CAMPAIGN OF 1847

It was thus in circumstances of political and social effervescence that the 1847 Banquet campaign opened in July when parliament went into its usual recession until December. The campaign was organised by the central committee of the Seine that had helped radicals gain seats in parliament. They consulted the English radical Cobden, a veteran of popular campaigning who was on a visit to Paris. On the advice of the republican publisher, Pagnerre, they planned a series of banquets and a mass petition, as in 1840. Only a minority of the 170 deputies who had voted for Rémusat's bill took part; Rémusat, Thiers and Dufaure dismissed the plan as illegal. The first banquet, at Château-Rouge in Paris, attracted 1,180 subscribers. The early banquets were moderate affairs, run by the *gauche dynastique*. The most sought-after speaker was Odilon Barrot. The Seine group encouraged sympathetic deputies to organise local banquets and provided a list of willing orators. Local notables, deputies, mayors, members of departmental general councils, were always prominent speakers. In 1847, 16 departmental councils voted in favour of electoral reform and held local banquets.

Initially, Ledru-Rollin and *La Réforme* had denigrated the Banquets as too timid, but by November, when 22 had been held, a more radical tone began to be heard and radicals began to compete with moderates for control of the campaign. Ledru-Rollin spoke in Lille on 7 November, to the displeasure of moderates. He roundly supported a democratic franchise and reforms to help the working man [*Doc. 45*]. On 21 November, along with Louis Blanc and Arago, he praised universal suffrage, the sovereignty of the people and the Convention in an address to an audience of 1,300. Speakers began to urge participants to raise their glasses to the socialist toast, 'the right to work'. At the end of the month the fourierist editor of *La Démocratie Pacifique*, Victor Considérant, a member of the departmental council in the Seine, told banqueteers that parliamentary reform was urgently needed to avoid popular disorder [41].

When parliament reassembled at the end of December 1847, the king criticised the campaign for its disloyal and blind tendencies and de Tocqueville spoke of his alarm at the government's failure to take account of social problems [*Doc. 46*]. By February 1848, 70 banquets had been held involving 22,000 subscribers and 100 deputies. Traditionally radical departments predominated; 28 in total, in the Paris area, the Nord, Saône and Rhône. Perhaps four times as many people listened to the speeches as subscribed to each banquet and, as always, the presence of local officials was noted with disquiet.

Up to the recall of parliament there had been some obstruction, but no attempt to ban any banquet, although local newspapers which reported the event enthusiastically were likely to be prosecuted. Tocqueville's speech was brushed aside in favour of a complex debate on foreign affairs. On 7 February the government suggested that future banquets could be stopped, using a 1790 law. This provoked Ledru-Rollin to quote the Jacobin Declaration of the Rights of Man of 1793, which he claimed defended the right of assembly as a natural right [*Doc. 48*]. A conservative amendment to the king's speech asking for an electoral reform proposal from the government was rejected by the narrowest margin to that date, 222 to 189, but a loyal acceptance of the speech, including Louis-Philippe's criticism of the Banqueteers, went through with 241 votes to three.

Although the Banquet 'season' had been successful as a series of conscious-raising events, successive banquets exacerbated divisions among reformers. Some, like Barrot wanted no more than minor modifications to the electoral laws, others wanted to re-organise electoral districts, some, notably the cohort from *Le National,* were in favour of universal male suffrage; the most extreme of these dreamt of a republic. Others wanted political reform to be tied in with social legislation. On the far left were socialists. They had imagined a variety of projects from the total re-structuring of society in the name of equality to people like Louis Blanc, who pushed the case for state loans to the unemployed and Victor Considérant, who wanted government public works expanded to recognise a 'right to work' for all. To square the circle, some socialists thought a republic was preferable to a monarchy. The Banquet campaign had exposed the deep division among reformers. The parliamentary vote showed that their unprecedented efforts had not increased their support. The desire to retain political power for a small elite was indicated by the absence, in most cases, of links between popular unrest sparked by economic issues and the suffrage movement. In Britain, the Chartist movement was fundamentally artisan in impetus; in France, the Banquet campaign was mostly run by, and for, a small elite. It was not the campaign that brought down Louis-Philippe, but the response of the Orleanists.

The Banquets continued, including the most radical so far, a communist gathering in Limoges, run by the utopian socialist, Théodore Bac. Ledru-Rollin threatened to revive the 1830 liberal scheme to persuade people to withhold taxation until the government agreed to a reform programme. A republican banquet, jointly organised by *La Réforme* and the 12th legion of the National Guard in the worker district of Saint-Marcel (Latin Quarter) was postponed on the order of the police until 22 February. Ledru-Rollin was invited, but withdrew when 80 other deputies said they would not go if he did. To mollify the government, the price of a ticket was raised from three to six francs and the organisers agreed both to restrict participation to voters and to re-locate the banquet out of the district. When *La Réforme* announced that the banquet would be preceded by a march of students and unemployed, the government banned it totally. The government feared the innovation of a fusion of economic grievance and franchise reform.

After an acrimonious debate in the offices of the newspaper, the organisers agreed by a large majority to cancel the banquet. Despite their desire for change, after more than half a century of repeated upheaval, few members of the educated elite actually believed that revolution was the way forward. Nearly all wanted to put pressure on the government, not overthrow the regime.

THE FEBRUARY REVOLUTION, 1848

The march went ahead, disowned, as were other worker and student demonstrations during the July Monarchy, by those thought of as potential leaders. From 8am on 22 February groups from worker districts, traditional and new, St Denis, St Martin, Temple, Belleville and Ménilmontant, converged on the place de la Madeleine. Here they were joined by students from the Latin Quarter. Their presence was partly an attempt to put pressure on the government to take positive steps to help the unemployed. Aware of criticism in the faculties and *grandes écoles*, part a matter of philosophical debate, part support for radical social, political and nationalist ideas, including sympathy for the Poles in rebellion against Russia, the Orleanists responded, like the Bourbons, with their version of 'thought police'. Popular courses given by Michelet, Quinet and the Polish patriot, Mickiewicz, were withdrawn. At the beginning of the year 3,000 students took to the streets when they heard that Michelet's lectures had been cancelled [32; 34].

The demonstrators marched, as planned, to the Palais Bourbon. Extra troops had been summoned to halt them. Apparently firing began without prior orders and fighting developed. Barricades began to go up haphazardly in neighbouring streets and there were calls for the government to resign [*Doc. 47*]. There was no indication on the first day that the march was any more threatening to the regime than had been numerous other similar events in the previous 18 years. A warning sign was that few of the National Guardsmen, called out to reinforce the troops, turned out for duty. Someone ought to have recalled that the cancelled banquet was organised by one of their most radical legions and that one of many reform projects over the years had been the enfranchisement of all guardsmen.

On 23 February the almost universal commitment of the National Guard to the Banquet campaign was evident and at midday Louis-Philippe was persuaded by the even more evident hostility to Guizot to replace him with Molé. Barrot, for the moment accepted as the mouthpiece of protest by the National Guard, welcomed the decision and asked the crowds to disperse. However Molé, a 70-year-old well-seasoned Orleanist minister, was an unlikely guarantor of reform. Crowds continued to mass and towards the evening marched on the Ministry of Foreign Affairs. Troops blocked their route. In the ensuing combat 52 people were killed and 74 injured.

Confrontation continued during the night. Trying to learn from his cousin's inaction in 1830, the king dumped Molé in favour of Thiers. The process of barricade building continued and by the morning of

24 February 1,500 had been erected and armourer's shops looted for weapons and ammunition. Louis-Philippe made the same mistake as his predecessor, putting an officer in to calm the situation whose presence was bound to do the opposite. This was marshal Bugeaud, a specialist in brutal repression. Demoralised at the sight of so many armed National Guardsmen defending the barricades, his officers and men began to change sides, just as they had done in 1830. Enlisted soldiers had little taste for guerilla warfare, which involved shooting women, children and families uncomfortably reminiscent of their own, manning makeshift barricades around their own homes.

By lunchtime on 24 February the king's palace in central Paris, the Tuileries, had been taken by the crowds. Louis-Philippe, displaying far more courage than his cousin, tried a similar tactic; he abdicated in favour of his nine-year old grandson, the comte de Paris. However crowds had moved on, in traditional fashion, to the parliament building, where parliament was hastily debating a regency under the duchesse d'Orléans, a liberal like her dead husband. Sensing that the monarchists had lost control, a small cohort of deputies, active in the Banquet campaign, and representing the two radical papers, particularly at this stage the more moderate, *Le National*, went on to the traditional practice of nominating themselves as a provisional government. These included Dupont de l'Eure, Ledru-Rollin, Lamartine, Arago, Crémieux, Marie and Garnier-Pagès.

All the best revolutions needed the sanction of the main *hôtel-de-ville,* and these men were well-versed in revolutionary tradition. There they met artisans from the surrounding streets and other journalists, speaking for *La Réforme.* More radical and socialist candidates were added to the list, Flocon, Louis Blanc and the mechanic Albert, head of the rump of the Society of the Seasons. They were all made secretaries of this self-appointed provisional government, together with Marrast, editor of *Le National.*

The new provisional government immediately declared the constitutional monarchy at an end, and proclaimed France a democratic republic. They gave the vote to all nine million adult males and speedy elections were promised for a Constituent Assembly which would write a new constitution. The republicans were determined to show people that they had no intention of smuggling the revolution away, as they claimed Orleanists had done in 1830. To reassure people who might fear that this Second Republic would mean a new Terror, they also abolished the death penalty for political crimes. A number of the republicans, of whom Louis Blanc was the noisiest, insisted that their new republic should also display its 'social' credentials, committing it to major social, as well as political, reform. Thus the republic was declared as 'democratic' and 'social'; employment was guaranteed [32; 34].

To take the story of the Second Republic further, readers should turn to the excellent volumes in this *Seminar Studies* series written by Peter Jones and William H. C. Smith on *The 1848 Revolutions, The Second Empire and Commune: France 1848–1871.*

10 WHAT DID REVOLUTION SIGNIFY? A COMPARISON OF 1830 AND 1848

Why were two monarchies eliminated within 18 years? It has been suggested that Charles X committed political suicide, failing to take advantage of the possibilities of compromise. The same cannot be said of Louis-Philippe. He remained in central Paris, in close touch with the crisis and took pains to learn from his cousin's mistakes. At 75 years of age he was accused of being doddery and dithering. He might have dismissed the Soult–Guizot government sooner, but in February 1848 the government was at its strongest in parliament, in contrast with 1830 when Polignac had no hope of majority support. Louis-Philippe's personal courage and determination, and his willingness to make changes during the days of revolution were to no avail.

Both political crises were conflicts over who should change the constitution. In 1830 the king and his chosen government were at odds with the liberal majority in parliament. The king claimed that the Four Ordinances were designed to check a threat of liberal insurrection and were within the letter of the constitution. In fact they were ultra manipulations, similar to repeated ultra legislation since 1820, altering the letter and defying the spirit of the constitution written in 1814. The Four Ordinances were a new departure; they were decree law, parliament was ignored. The polarisation of politics in 1830 was far more due to the king than the liberals. The removal of the ultra ministers and the appointment of more centrist royalists would have averted the political crisis.

In 1848 king, ministers and the majority in parliament were in accord. The political conflict was between them and a vocal minority in parliament, which, in the weeks before the February revolution, had begun to make common cause with popular unrest. The decision to combine the two groups with a march and banquet in Paris on 23 February could have been avoided by both protagonists. The government could have introduced modest electoral reform, for instance the enfranchisement of 100-franc taxpayers, the more educated and prestigious of whom already voted by right, and many of whom were already voting to make up minimum numbers in poorer constituencies. Thwarted and out-voted in parliament, their most radical critics had deliberately chosen to take constitutional issues on to the streets, and were keen to cite the right to rebellion in the Jacobin Constitution of 1793.

Why did confrontation develop and why were compromises not made? The essence of the constitutions, 1814 and 1830, was that issues such as ministerial responsibility had been left vague, leaving adequate scope for negotiation. Electoral laws could be modified through parliament with comparative ease. In 1830 and 1848, both rulers and their governments misjudged the seriousness of their position and failed to take action which might have contained unrest. One is tempted to think both were *too* conscious of the past. They interpreted the escalation of revolution in the early 1790s as being fuelled by the willingness to make concessions. Both rulers seemed to forget that since 1814, if not 1793, the presence of a monarch had been a matter of convenience and negotiation among the political elite, not principle. Politicians made their monarchs in 1814 and in 1830. A king was an arbiter, not an autocrat. Yet the politicians failed to take account of the tenuous and contractual nature of royal power when they wrote constitutions. Once a monarch had been appointed, the written record, the constitution, whether that of 1814 or 1830, accorded the ruler full executive rights, including the right to make war and peace, a share in law-making, and the right to appoint ministers without consulting parliament.

WHY COMPROMISE DID NOT WORK

The constitutional monarchies depended on a basic level of consent. In neither regime was the opportunity to weigh and consider serious dissent envisaged in practice. Indeed, the parameters of dissent were constantly narrowed in both regimes, by censorship and by laws against Associations. The National Guard and army were relied upon to maintain the shrinking area between order and revolution. Why were both regimes unable to countenance criticism? Why did 'Order' have to mean the denial of discussion? Why was there a tendency to ideological autocracy? Rousseau's doctrine of the General Will might be seen as the culprit, or the intolerance of the Robespierrist concept of Republican Virtue and the Terror. In real life, ultras and liberals worked together to promote liberty of the press in the 1820s and Orleanists and their left-wing critics sat together in the Academy of

Moral and Political Sciences. The notables, ultra and Orleanist, could tolerate each other. However, all were afraid of 'the popular classes'. The explanation for the instability of nineteenth-century regimes, monarchist or republican, was the fear of the elites that the 'masses' were always ready to overturn the established social, economic and political order and the willingness of their most radical critics to threaten to unleash 'the dangerous classes'.

This apprehension was based on the memory and myth of the 1790s, the proliferation of popular unrest in their own day and the assumption that 'class war' was a real threat (or a manageable ally). At base this notion was rooted in ignorance and contemporary notions of human biology. The disenfranchised poor were the 'other', a different species, a race of untouchables. The lines of demarcation between the races were vividly described in contemporary novels [*Doc. 7*]. They were marked by the arbitrarily defined levels of wealth required for voters, parallel education systems which excluded the poor from the professions and social advance and, in the final analysis, written in blood by military force. It must have come as quite a shock in April 1848 to find that the 'popular classes' voted for a conservative Assembly, and in December for a Bonaparte.

The reluctance of government critics to press their advantage and actually play the card of popular insurrection was apparent in both July 1830 and February 1848. During the Three Glorious Days, liberal journalists and politicians were divided and indecisive. On 22 February 1848, the reformers were even more split than they had been when the Banquet campaign started, and when the government banned the Paris banquet the reformers concurred. Why then did confrontation flip over into revolution? Two interconnecting factors seemed to have been conclusive in both revolutions. The first was military, the second social geography.

THE ROLE OF THE NATIONAL GUARD AND THE ARMY IN REVOLUTION

When the artisan and student demonstrations began, the Parisian National Guard took the rebel side on both occasions. As riots turned to revolution in 1848, the regiments on duty went over to the rebels, just as they had in 1830.

Why? The defections of 1830 have often been linked with Bonapartist sympathies among National Guardsmen and regular troops. Given the 18-year gap, was such an explanation relevant in 1848? It may have been; Louis-Napoleon was elected to the National Assembly in

June 1848 by an artisan constituency in Paris. However, the explanation may lie rather in the nature of the conflict and the social geography of central Paris. The successful construction of barricades across the narrow streets of artisan quarters, built partly with domestic objects and manned by families, including women and children, were a unique feature of nineteenth-century revolution. The ensuing conflict was an urban guerilla warfare in which regular troops were asked to fire, at close quarters, on families like their own. Perhaps it was less political identification than simple human identification which caused the troops to desert. In 1830, there were other practical factors. The soldiers knew that they were out-numbered and ill-provisioned compared with their assailants. Reinforcements and new supplies of ammunition never arrived. Worse, on hot July days there were no arrangements to feed and water soldiers; the families of their protagonists had sometimes dined – and wined – them.

In 1848, the implementation of Thiers's plan to build a ring of forts around the capital and the use of railways for transport meant that reinforcements could be secured far more easily than in 1830, but the defections were just as rapid. Commentators noted on both occasions that the two army commanders, Marmont and Bugeaud, were unpopular. The structure of the army may have played a part, composed as it was by a privileged officer corps and a conscript mass, with consequent mistrust and misunderstanding.

REVOLUTION AND SOCIAL GEOGRAPHY

In the final resort, perhaps the social geography of the capital, combined with the erection of barricades in residential areas, were the most significant factors in both 1830 and 1848. Paris had almost doubled in population since 1830 but, although new districts had been created, the centre of government and the heart of artisan Paris remained cheek by jowl, and therefore difficult to control once a demonstration began to explode [78; 197]. Paris was the heart of a highly centralised state, yet the nerve-centre of government. The houses of its wealthy political elite were within a stone's throw of crowded artisan quarters, into which more and more workers were crammed in these years. This volatile combination was made even more explosive by the presence in the same streets of newspapers, the most successful of which were always hostile to the established regime. Added to this, the volcanic right-bank centre of Paris had been the stamping ground for the events of the 1790s; buildings, like the Hôtel-de-Ville, the Palais Royal, the Tuileries, etc., had become icons of revolution. The experience of repeated political upheaval in the 1790s had educated the French to accept the right of popular insurrection to challenge accepted authority. Since 1830 the Jacobin Declaration of Rights with its clause sanctifying the right to rebel had been part of the republican catechism, and the majority of Parisian republicans were artisans living and working in these districts [*Doc. 48*].

Just as in 1830, in 1848 there was no united alternative waiting to replace the defeated regime. Parliament contained no more than half a dozen convinced republicans and when the journalists of the two main radical papers were added, it was apparent that there was no consensus, particularly on social reform. Louis Blanc was given the job of running a commission of workers and employers at the Luxembourg Palace, but few of his colleagues in the provisional government supported his ideas for social workshops. He was kept completely isolated from the National Workshops themselves. In the following months these workshops tried to employ over 100,000 unemployed in the capital alone, and many thousands in other cities, but the majority of the provisional government was determined that these should not be the prototype of Blanc-style social workshops, but a temporary expedient, modelled on past experience. As always after a revolution, the economic crisis worsened and the provisional government felt obliged to adopt unpopular emergency taxes to keep afloat. Universal male suffrage was a disaster for the republicans. The new electorate voted in an assembly of 'notables', most of them wealthy enough and monarchist enough to have sat in the parliaments of the defeated regime, which many of them had. After some hesitation the Assembly tried to break up the National Workshops. The result was the June Days, when Parisian artisans rebelled to protect their 'right to work' as an integral part of the 'social republic'. The rebellion terrified moderate republicans and the scale of military repression disgusted the working population. All that remained of republican dreams was the nightmare that universal male suffrage proved to be the means by which Louis-Napoleon was elected president in December.

11 CONCLUSION: WRITING THE HISTORY OF THE CONSTITUTIONAL MONARCHY

Historians have never had much time for the constitutional monarchy. Even a Catholic monarchist historian like Bertier de Sauvigny described the July Ordinances as a *coup d'état* [3; 46]. The Third Republic historian, Thureau-Dangin, was almost alone in his enthusiasm for Guizot and the Orleanists [191]. The years of constitutional monarchy have been dismissed as a hiatus by historians, influenced by the utopian scorn of the socialists and the supercilious superiority of republicans. The monarchies have been derided because they failed to create permanent regimes, because French nationalist interests were neglected and because they, and particularly the Orleanists, took insufficient account of the 'social question' and thus left France prey to increasing social conflicts, especially the June Days.

According to the French republican history-writing tradition which evolved during the Third Republic (1870–1940), the constitutional monarchy was never more than a staging-post on the way back to a republic. The republican historians of the Third Republic were socialists, including the socialist leader in parliament before 1914, Jaurès. They saw themselves as heirs of a Jacobin tradition. Their argument rested on twin pillars. First, that the Jacobin constitution of the First Republic offered both a democratic and a social-reforming model, and secondly, that class conflicts inherent in economic changes in the nineteenth century were bound to lead from an aristocratic, to a bourgeois, to a proletarian society. They adopted Marx's interpretation of the Orleanist monarchy as a regime of bourgeois bankers and businessmen, which would inevitably be toppled in the course of capitalist development when the masses rose against economic deprivation engineered by an increasingly wealthy, but shrinking, bourgeoisie. In recent years much of this economic-determinist argument has been questioned [115]. Detailed regional analysis, *de rigueur* for doctoral theses in the 1960s and 1970s, revealed that popular unrest was far more of an endemic than a particular issue in these years and that rioters had their own specific agendas within a generic revolutionary rhetoric [102; 121; 126]. Some historians have been reluctant to abandon the notion that a class-conscious proletariat was developing in these years [116; 134]. Many have been relieved to demonstrate that early socialism was dominated by traditional artisan ideas and organisations [32; 37; 85; 104; 128; 129; 144; 157; 174; 180].

The student of the constitutional monarchy is thus likely to encounter quite distinct approaches to this period. In accounts written before 1960 one reads an interpretation which categorises 1830 as a take-over by a wealthy financial elite, 1848 the triumph of a lesser bourgeoisie, followed in June 1848 by the first proletarian revolution. Then there were empiricists, like Cobban, who described both 1830 and February 1848 as 'accidental' or avoidable revolutions, the product of the coincidence of political and economic crises [58]. More recently, in the hands of Agulhon, Margadant, Merriman, Price and others, both revolutions have been seen in a longer perspective, in the context of popular upheaval reaching from the defeat of Napoleon to the Second Republic (1848–52) and beyond [32; 34; 121; 129; 153].

After the Second World War, another war was waged by the *Annales* school, clustered around an influential periodical of the same name, which has impacted on approaches to all periods of French history. Their condemnation of historical writing that listed just one political event after another, encouraged historians of the nineteenth century to try to expand their perspective on the past, using anthropology and psychology, as well as statistical and cultural sources. Marc Bloch, one of the founders of *annaliste* history, insisted that historians should look up from the written archives to study the topography of the land, the architecture of the city. Historians were encouraged to shun the history of limited periods, circumscribed by politics, and to look at much longer time-spans to explore social change, using modern computers and earlier adding machines to probe otherwise intractable statistical data such as wills and electoral lists. Adèline Daumard and André-Jean Tudesq offered us magisterial studies, the one of the bourgeoisie, the other of the notables [63; 194]. Historians have also learned to be sceptical of nineteenth-century statistics and the lack of adequate comparable data [42]. Others escaped from statistics into contemporary literature and discovered the dangers of taking contemporary novelists at face value. Louis Chevalier's moving account of the Paris poor has since been criticised for its lack of critical perspective because he took contemporary novelists at face value [55]. While the adult male, rich or poor, still dominates histories of the early nineteenth century, since the 1970s the contribution of women, particularly radicals, from saint-simonians to socialists, has begun to be studied [83; 86; 114; 132; 133; 142; 164; 187].

In recent years, perhaps following Bloch's advice, historians have taken an interest in many aspects of material culture, and Marrinan, Weisberg, Chu and others have produced revealing studies of artists and lithographers, providing fresh insights into how the artist (and his patron) may have influenced their contemporaries, a task made easier by cheaper photographic reproduction of paintings, drawings, etc. Buildings, statues, monuments, now feature in our much more vivid visual impressions of the constitutional monarchy [33; 120; 197].

As French historians began to question the previously dominant Marxist approach, they tended to revert to the world of ideas, in particular to those of the Enlightenment and the nineteenth-century liberals. In the process, they have begun to see more of value in these years, noting the 'apprenticeship' in parliamentary government, the gradual development of the economy and the flowering of cultural life, although there have been no voices raised to contradict the basic faith that the future was republican. This period provides a rich variety of original voices for the historian. Throughout this volume references to novels, paintings, lithographs, etc. are woven into the text. However, it is the self-reliant determination of individuals, from seamstresses to millionaires, to try to solve the inequities in their society and not to leave it to others which holds this writer's attention. I am encouraged to search out more examples of tiny schools, nurseries, evening classes, free clinics, which in totality diminished the relevance of the posturing elites of monarchy and notables.

PART FOUR: DOCUMENTS

All translations by the author, unless otherwise indicated.

DOCUMENT 1   THE PREAMBLE TO THE CONSTITUTIONAL
            CHARTER 4 JUNE 1814

Divine Providence, in recalling us to our land after a long absence, has imposed great obligations on us. Peace was the prime need of our subjects; we have concentrated on it without a break; and this Peace settlement, as necessary to France as to the rest of Europe, has now been signed. Circumstances within the country cried out for a constitutional charter; we concurred and herewith publish it. We have taken account that, although all power rests in the person of the king, from time to time our predecessors have not hesitated in modifying how that power was exercised. ... [W]e have understood that the desire of our subjects for a constitutional charter was the expression of a real need. ... While we recognise that a free and monarchical constitution will be very acceptable to enlightened opinion in Europe, we have also taken into account that our first duty to our people is, in their interests, to conserve the rights and prerogatives of our crown. ... Above all we want Frenchmen to live as brothers. ... Thus willingly, and by the free exercise of our royal authority, we have granted this constitutional charter to our subjects.

L. Duguit and H. Monnier, [12], pp. 183–4.

DOCUMENT 2   CONSTITUTIONAL CHARTER, 4 JUNE 1814

Public law of the French

1. The French are equal before the law, whatever their titles or rank.
2. They contribute, without distinction, according to their fortune, to the expenses of the state.
3. All are equally admissable to civil and military jobs.
4. Their individual liberty is guaranteed, no one can be arrested except in cases provided by the law and according to legally accepted practices.
5. Everyone shall practise their religion with equal liberty and all religions shall have the same protection.

6. The Roman Catholic, apostolic religion shall be the religion of the state.
7. The ministers of the Roman Catholic apostolic religion and those of other Christian faiths, shall be paid a salary by the state.
8. The French have the right to publish their opinions and have them printed, according to laws which are designed to deal with abuses of this freedom.
9. All property is inviolable, including that which is called *national property*, and the law makes no distinction between them.
10. The state may demand the sacrifice of property if it is in the public interest, but an indemnity must be paid.
11. There may be no investigations into opinions and votes recorded before the Restoration.
12. Conscription is abolished. The method of recruitment for army and navy will be determined by law.

Forms of the King's Government

13. The person of the king is inviolable and sacred. His ministers are responsible. Executive power belongs to him.
14. The king is the supreme head of state, he is the commander of the army and navy, declares war, makes treaties of peace, alliance and trade, appoints all public officials, and makes whatever regulations and ordinances are required for the execution of laws and the security of the state.
15. Legislative power belongs collectively to the king, the chamber of peers and the chamber of deputies of the department.
16. The king proposes laws.
17. Proposals for laws are considered, on the initiative of the king, by the chamber of peers or chamber of deputies, except tax laws, which must go first to the chamber of deputies.
18. All laws must secure a majority in both houses of parliament.
19. Both houses have the right to ask the king to propose legislation, and to ask that laws remain in force.
20. Either chamber may make this request, after secret debate; the decision will be sent to the other chamber after a 10-day delay.
21. If the king rejects their joint proposal, it cannot be discussed again during the same session.
22. The king sanctions and promulgates laws.
23. The civil list is fixed by parliament in the first session of each reign.

Duguit and Monnier, [12], pp. 184–6.

DOCUMENT 3   EXTRACT FROM STENDHAL'S *SCARLET AND BLACK*

Stendhal's Scarlet and Black *was published in 1830. Its hero, Julien Sorel, has inherited his father's Bonapartism, carries Napoleon's memoirs in his knapsack, and becomes a priest (the 'black') during the Restoration, rather than join the army ('the red'), in which ambitious young lads could hope to make their name under the Emperor.*

In his earliest childhood he had been violently attracted to the military profession by the sight of certain dragoons of the 6th regiment returning from Italy, in long white cloaks, and helmets with long black plumes of horsehair on their heads, whom he had seen tying up their horses to the iron-barred window of his father's house. Later on, he had listened, entranced, to tales of battles at the bridge of Lodi, at Arcola and Rivoli, told him by the old army surgeon, and he had seen the old man's eyes flash as he glanced at his cross.

But when Julien was fourteen, they were beginning to build a church at Verrières, one that could be termed magnificent for so small a town. ... All at once Julien stopped talking about Napoleon. He announced his plan of becoming a priest, and was constantly to be seen in his father's sawmill, busy committing to memory a Latin Bible which the curé had lent him. ... For Julien, achieving success meant first and foremost getting away from Verrières ... he revelled in dreams of being one day introduced to beautiful Parisian women. ... Why should he not be loved by one of them, just as Bonaparte, when still poor, had been loved by that distinguished lady, Madame de Beauharnais? For many years past Julien had not let perhaps a single hour go by without telling himself that Bonaparte, an unknown penniless lieutenant, had made himself master of the world with his sword ...

When Bonaparte, he thought, made people talk about him, France lived in fear of invasion. Military ability was an essential need, and it became the fashion. Today we see priests only forty years old with stipends of a hundred thousand francs – that is to say, three times as much as Napoleon's famous major-generals. These priests must have people who back them up. Look at that justice of the peace, for instance, such a decent fellow and such an honorable man up till now, and so old too, committing a dishonourable act for fear of displeasing a young cleric of thirty. I must become a priest.

Stendhal, [27], pp. 42–4.

DOCUMENT 4   ANGE GUÉPIN DESCRIBES URBAN POVERTY

Ange Guépin (1805–73) was a saint-simonian doctor in Nantes who took a lead in the July Days in the city. In 1835 he published, in collaboration with a colleague, the first graphic description of urban squalor.

Beyond the scrap of bread he needs to support his family, and the bottle of wine with which he forgets his sorrows, the worker sees nothing and aspires to nothing. If you want to know how he lives ... enter, bowing your head before one of the open sewers ... the air is as cold and humid as in a cellar; your feet slip about on the filthy ground; and you are afraid of falling into the mire. On either side of the alley, which slopes below ground level, is a dark, large, frozen room, dirty water oozing from the walls, with scant air reaching it from a window, too small to let in any light, and so badly-fitting that it will not fasten. ... There are two or three beds, roughly held together with string ... occasionally sheets and a pillow. As for cupboards, no one has need of them. Sometimes you will find a spinning wheel or a loom. ... By the age of twenty people are thriving or already dead.

A. Guépin and C.E. Bonamy, *Nantes au XIXe siècle*, Nantes, 1835. Quoted in L. Blanc, *Organisation du Travail*, edited by J. A. R. Marriot, *The French Revolution of 1848 in its Economic Aspect*, vol. 1, Oxford, 1913, pp. 38–9.

DOCUMENT 5   **DR VILLERMÉ ON A WORKER'S BUDGET**

Dr. Villermé (1782–1863) first practised as an army doctor and then became a specialist commentator on contemporary medicine and society. He was commissioned to report on working conditions by the Académie des Sciences Morales et Politiques, *of which he was a member.*

Among the three industries which have been the focus of my research, cotton spinners and weavers are the worst off. Women are worst paid of all, not only in an absolute sense, but also relative to their needs; they can only make ends meet by being brutally economical and depriving themselves of basic necessities. Those who can't resist fancy clothes are likely to be drawn into immoral behaviour to pay the bills.

The main element in the worker's budget is food, made up as follows: For a man, at least half, maybe two-thirds to three-quarters, if he drinks. A woman will spend a half to two-thirds of her money on food, an adolescent three-quarters. The cost is less per head in a family, but a father who passes his time at the *cabaret* will spend as much on himself as on his whole family.

After food, comes clothing, which with laundry bills makes up between an eighth and a quarter of total costs; rent comes to between a twelfth and a tenth, more in large industrial towns where the poor often have to pay rents as high as those in Paris.

L. R. Villermé, [30], vol. 2, pp. 21–2.

DOCUMENT 6   A COMPARISON OF POVERTY IN FRANCE
                AND ENGLAND

In 1840 Eugène Buret (1810–42) was awarded a prize by the Académie des
Sciences Morales et Politiques, *for his comparison of poverty in France and
England. Statistics were a novel and admired feature of the work.*

There are in France 1,329 hospitals and asylums for 40,000 communes. In
1833 these establishments admitted 425,029 persons belonging to the class of
the really poor. In France the people who go into a hospital to die really are
driven there by poverty. ... The welfare committees, which distribute aid to
recognised paupers in their homes, assisted 695,932 persons during the same
year 1833. ... The number of persons officially listed as paupers was, therefore, in 1833, 1,120,961; which gives a ratio of 1 official pauper in every
29.021 of the population. ... Assuming that each official pauper represents at
least three actual paupers, the number 1,120,961 assisted persons gives us a
mass of human suffering which must amount to 1 in every 9.673 of the total
population.

E. Buret, [8], in Collins, [10], pp. 140–1.

DOCUMENT 7   THE 'DANGEROUS CLASSES'

*The poor were all the 'dangerous classes' and a race apart for the middle
classes who enjoyed Victor Hugo's Les Misérables. Novelists like Hugo convinced their readers that among the poor family and moral values did not exist.*

A quite young girl was standing in the open doorway, facing the pallid light of
the one small window in Marius's garret, which was opposite the door. ... The
light fell upon reddened hands, a stringy neck, a loose depraved mouth lacking several teeth, bleared eyes both bold and wary; in short, an ill-treated girl
with the eyes of a grown woman; a blend of fifty and fifteen; one of those
creatures, at once weak and repellent, who cause those who set eyes on them
to shudder when they do not weep ...

   People reduced to the last extremity of need are also driven to the utmost
limit of their resources, and woe to any defenceless person who comes their
way. Work and wages, food and warmth, courage and goodwill – all this is
lost to them. The daylight dwindles into shadow and darkness enters their
hearts; and within this darkness man seizes upon the weakness of woman and
child and forces them into ignominy. No horror is then excluded. Desperation
is bounded only by the flimsiest of walls, all giving access to vice and crime.

   Health and youth, honour and the sacred, savage delicacy of still-young
flesh, truth of heart, virginity, modesty, those protective garments of the soul,
all are put to the vilest of uses in the blind struggle for survival that must
encounter, and submit to, every outrage ...

To Marius the girl was in some sort an emissary of that underworld, disclosing a hideous aspect of its darkness.

V. Hugo, [17], pp. 633–9.

DOCUMENT 8   EXTRACT FROM SUZANNE VOILQUIN'S
MEMOIRS

Suzanne Voilquin (1810–77) joined the saint-simonians and edited the first newspaper for women, La Femme Libre *(1832–33). She always described herself as a daughter of the people, although her father had been a comfortably-off hatter, hit by economic crisis. She and her sister did embroidery. During an eventful, much-travelled life, she learned and practised midwifery and homeopathy. She wrote her memoirs when she was aged 67.*

Our only room, on the third storey, had a single window that looked out on a narrow and sombre courtyard. Just the sight of the house wrung our hearts. When we returned from work in the evening and had to cross that dark alley, and holding hands, climb that foul-smelling stairway to reach our room, we would experience insane terrors …

In this period, we also made acquaintance of what is most painful in the life of a worker: *unemployment*. It was the end of the reign of Louis the Desired [Louis XVIII]. Everywhere the luxury trades had ground to a halt, for the decorum of the court demanded dreariness. Balls and celebrations were proscribed. No more of those gold and silver-spangled dresses, nor those delicious whims of fancy which, even as they adorned the privileged beauties, at least provided a livelihood for the working woman. Mrs. Martin's workshop was reduced by three-fourths. Since we were the last to be hired, we were the first to be let go. … All I was able to find were job lots of embroidery that were very badly paid, but we had to accept them or die of starvation. We rented looms and worked in our room. During those two months, the most we earned in a day was *one* franc for each of us, and that required beginning at six in the morning and keeping at it, often until midnight.

S. Voilquin, [31], in Trangott, [29], p. 114.

DOCUMENT 9   ARTISAN ORGANISATIONS AT WORK

Agricol Perdiguier (1805–75) was probably the most famous artisan of his day, a qualified joiner, like his father, who set up his own craft school in Paris and wrote extensively about artisan organisations and the need for them to co-operate with each other. 'Worker' culture was briefly fashionable among middle-class socialists, who argued that a self-taught man like Perdiguier was nearer to God than more sophisticated and wealthy folk like them. Perdiguier learned to exploit this to his advantage.

The *compagnonnage* had many members and was very active in Nantes. Battles among *compagnons* were also frequent. Since the terrible combat between *gavots* and blacksmiths, which cost the life of one smith, other disorders have taken place.

Nantes is the headquarters city for *compagnon* nail makers. Members of this occupation stand out because of their number, their dress, and the nature of their ceremonies. They preside over their assemblies, or did then, in high hats and knee breeches. They wear ponytails and pigtails on the back of their heads. When one of their brothers is buried, they untie their hair and let it hang, wave, fly about their necks and in front of their faces, however the breeze blows it ...

Compagnon nail makers are very charitable. They provide fraternal support to one another. If a *compagnon* is on the road and finds himself without work, what does he do? He goes to the first nail maker's shop he finds along his path and explains his difficulties. One of the workers will surrender his hammer and his place at the anvil, and go off and travel in turn, or else the new arrival is given assistance, which is not charity, but a loan.

Agricol Perdiguier, [21], in Traugott, [29], p. 155.

DOCUMENT 10   GUIZOT'S DEFENCE OF THE RESTORATION

François Guizot (1787–1874) was the son of a prosperous Protestant lawyer in Nîmes who backed the Girondins and was guillotined by the Jacobins. The son became professor of history at the Sorbonne in 1812, supported the 1814 Restoration and left France with Louis XVIII during the Hundred Days. Secretary-general of the Ministry of Justice at the Second Restoration, the ultra reaction after 1820 turned him into an opposition liberal and the organiser of Aide-toi. He became one of Louis-Philippe's longest-serving ministers. Here he explains why he accepted the Restoration.

I had no previous tie, no personal motive, to connect me with the Restoration; I sprang from those who had been raised up by the impulse of 1789, and who were little disposed to fall back again. But if I was not bound to the former system by any specific interest, I felt no bitterness towards the old government of France. Born a citizen and a Protestant, I have ever been unswervingly devoted to liberty of conscience, equality in the eyes of the law, and all the acquired privileges of social order. My confidence in these acquisitions is ample and confirmed; but in support of their cause, I do not feel myself called upon to consider the House of Bourbon, the aristocracy of France, and the Catholic clergy, as enemies.

F. Guizot, [16], vol. 1, pp. 27–8.

DOCUMENT 11   VICTOR COUSIN'S INAUGURAL LECTURE
AT THE SORBONNE

Victor Cousin (1792–1867) was the son of a poor Parisian watchmaker, delivered from the streets to an education in the lycée Charlemagne, *by the grateful family of a young lad he rescued from bullying. In 1810 he was one of the first students at the* Ecole Normale, *where, after three years, he was made a lecturer in philosophy and Greek. He moved to the Sorbonne in 1815, but his liberal ideas robbed him of his post between 1820 and 1827. After 1830, acknowledged as the leading philosopher of the age, he was made director of the* Ecole Normale *and a peer. His first lecture at the Sorbonne began*:

It is to those of you whose age is close to mine that I dare to speak at this moment; to you who will form the emerging generation; to you, the sole support, the last hope of our dear and unfortunate country. Gentlemen, you passionately love our fatherland; if you wish to save it, espouse our noble doctrines.

V. Cousin, 'Discours prononcé à l'ouverture de cours de l'histoire de la philosophie, 13 décembre 1815', in A. Spitzer, [186], pp. 91–2.

DOCUMENT 12   REBUILDING THE RESTORATION ARMY

Laurent Gouvion de Saint-Cyr (1764–1830), a marshal in 1812, was made a peer by Louis XVIII in 1814, refused to support the Hundred Days, and became Minister of War at the Second Restoration. He rebuilt the Restoration army and gave this speech on 26 January 1818.

We must decide whether there exists in our midst two armies, two nations, one of which will be struck with anathema, declared unfit to serve the king and France. And to stay within the bounds of what concerns me directly, we must decide whether we will once again call to the defence of the fatherland soldiers who have made its glory, or whether we will declare them once and for all dangerous to its tranquillity. The latter decision would be harsh and unjust, for these soldiers were admirable on the day of battle.

This speech was written for him by Guizot, reprinted in A. Jardin and A. J. Tudesq, [98] p. 37.

DOCUMENT 13   FOURIER'S SOCIAL HARMONY

Charles Fourier (1772–1837) was the son of a family of Besançon merchants, who earned his living as a traveling salesman and clerk, while writing a series of virtually unreadable accounts of his utopian vision of the future, when all the seas would be pink lemonade and everyone would grow long tails. He believed his experimental community was the answer to all contemporary problems.

Civilised nations, you are about to take a giant step forward in the social world. By passing directly into social harmony you are escaping twenty revolutions which could bathe the world in blood for another twenty centuries before the theory of the destinies were discovered.

Charles Fourier, [14], p. 34 and in Stedman Jones and Patterson (trans), p. 181.

DOCUMENT 14   THE ARCHBISHOP OF PARIS ADDRESSES HIS CONGREGATION, MAY 1830

Monseigneur de Quélen (1778–1839), son of a noble family, served the Imperial Church and became Archbishop of Paris in 1819. This was an address to his congregation in Notre-Dame, May 1830.

The lily banner, inseparable from the cross, will once more leave the field victorious ... if we never neglect any of the means which order our duty to obtain monarchical and religious elections. We have reason to be interested in a cause so legitimate to the God of Clotide and Saint Louis.

D. L. Rader, [154], pp. 208–9.

DOCUMENT 15   THE RESPONSE OF THE DEPUTIES TO THE SPEECH FROM THE THRONE AT THE OPENING OF THE 1830 SESSION

Sire, the people cherish and respect your authority. Fifteen years of peace and liberty that they owe to your august brother and yourself have deeply rooted in their hearts the gratitude which binds them to the royal family ...

Nevertheless, Sire, amid the unanimous feeling of respect and affection with which your people surround you there has grown up a spirit of uneasiness which ruffles the security that France has begun to enjoy and taints the sources of her prosperity. If it is prolonged, it could become fatal to her peace ...

Sire, the Charter that we owe to your august predecessor, and whose benefits your Majesty has firmly resolved to consolidate, consecrates as a right the intervention of the people in the deliberation of public concerns. This intervention must be, and indeed is, indirect, wisely restrained, confined within well-defined limits; but it is positive in its result, for it brings about permanent agreement between the political views of your government and the wishes of your people, which is the indispensable condition of the orderly conduct of public affairs. Sire, our loyalty and devotion force us to tell you that this agreement does not exist. The fundamental attitude of the government today is an unwarranted mistrust of the feelings and opinions of France.

Address of 221 deputies, 19 March 1830, translated in Collins, [10], p. 84.

DOCUMENT 16   CHARLES X'S RESPONSE TO THE ADDRESS OF THE 221 ON 19 MARCH 1830

This most recent Chamber of Deputies has deliberately misunderstood my intentions. I should be able to rely on its support in order to rule in the interests of my people; the Chamber has refused to support me. As father of my people, my soul was wounded, as king I was offended; the Chamber is thus dissolved.

A copy of the speech was sent to all prefects, Archives départementales, Puy-de-Dôme M62.

DOCUMENT 17   REPORT OF CHANTELAUZE, GARDE DES SCEAUX, TO THE KING, JULY 1830, JUSTIFYING THE ORDINANCES

Your ministers would not be worthy of your confidence if they delayed longer ... in calling to your attention how dangerous newspapers have become ... symptoms of anarchy are apparent everywhere, despite material prosperity. ... A virulent, ardent and indefatigable ill will threatens ... to stir up the popular classes ... the freedom of the press is to blame ... Newspapers have always been instruments of disorder and sedition ... they direct public opinion and try to dominate parliamentary debates ...

Existing laws have proved inadequate to restrain the press ... We must turn to the Charter ... article 14 gives your Majesty sufficient power, not only to change our institutions, but also to consolidate them and make them more secure.

Bertier de Sauvigny, [3], p. 31.

DOCUMENT 18   THE FOUR ORDINANCES OF JULY 1830

The freedom of the press is suspended ...
The Chamber of Deputies is dissolved ...
The new Chamber of Deputies will consist only of the deputies elected by the departmental colleges ...
Electoral colleges will meet on 6 and 13 of September ... parliament will reassemble on 28 September.

Bertier de Sauvigny, [3], pp. 37–42.

DOCUMENT 19   THE INDECISION OF THE LIBERAL JOURNALISTS

Charles de Rémusat (1797–1875), was the son of a notable lawyer who served all regimes, until Villèle dismissed him from his prefecture. In the 1820s Charles became a close friend of Adolphe Thiers and editor of the Globe.

26 July 1830. I was walking towards the rue Saint-Marc, where the offices of the *National* were located. I was on the hunt for news, and a bit of support. I ran into a large and noisy meeting, presided over by a man I didn't know, Treilhard. All our friends from the *National* were there, Thiers, Mignet, Carrel, Paulin and other journalists including Châtelain, Cauchois-Lemaire, Léon Pillet and so on. They were floundering around, getting nowhere; the room was full of people, all wanting to have their say. Thiers was determined that they should make a formal declaration of their resistance. He wasn't sure how to proceed; but was very keen that they all took a common line ...

It was a very hot day. There was some excellent iced orangeade on the table, which I drank while Thiers composed the protest.

Charles de Rémusat, *Mémoires de ma vie* (ed. C. H. Pouthas), 3 vols, Paris 1959, vol. 2, pp. 413–14.

DOCUMENT 20   THE PROTEST OF THE LIBERAL JOURNALISTS, 26 JULY 1830

In the last 10 months there has been a lot of talk about laws being broken and that a *coup d'état* was imminent. No one could credit such ideas. The government insisted it was all lies. However the *Moniteur* has now published these ordinances, which are an outrageous violation of the law. The rule of law is thus interrupted, the reign of force has begun.

In these circumstances, one is no longer committed to obedience. The first to be ordered to obey are journalists; thus they must be the first to resist ...

We shall try to publish and circulate our newspapers ... this is our duty as citizens. Today the government has lost the status of legality that commands obedience. We shall resist ... it is up to the rest of France to determine the form its resistance will take.

Bertier de Sauvigny, [3], pp. 59–61.

DOCUMENT 21   THE JULY REVOLUTION (1)

Odilon Barrot (1791–1873), a member of the Restoration judiciary who sided with the Bourbons in the Hundred Days, came from a family which had supported the Revolution. He was the defence council for numerous liberals in the 1820s, a moderate member of Aide-toi and a prominent organiser of the Banquet campaign of 1847. He wrote his memoirs late in life and they were not published until after his death.

At that time I lived in a house in the cloisters of Saint-Germain l'Auxerrois ... and my route home took me through central Paris, the Palais Royal, rue Saint-Honoré, the Louvre etc. Already [27th] people were agitated and large and menacing crowds were everywhere. Shops had taken down their signs displaying royal crests; patrols of soldiers had no sooner passed by than crowds had gathered again.

When I crossed the rue du Coq, I encountered a group of workers, carrying a makeshift stretcher bearing a work-mate with a bloody bayonet wound. They made off in the direction of the suburbs, crying out for vengeance: all the signs of a revolution were present.

When I reached home, I must confess with some embarrassment, now that age and experience has cooled my blood, I threw aside my books and notes and donned my National Guard uniform and set my secretaries to work to prepare ammunition ...

I was anxious to meet up with my comrades from the 4th legion. ... Shopkeepers had put up their shutters and were wearing their National Guard uniforms; but when I shouted to them to join me, they stayed in their doorways and replied that it was not in their interest. They had put on their uniforms to protect their businesses and no more. ... Just then another National Guard officer was shot in the stomach by one of the Swiss Guards on duty defending the Louvre. He died on the spot. The war had begun and frustrations exploded; those who had tried to stand aside were dragged into action.

Odilon Barrot, [2], vol. 1, pp. 102–3; also in Bertier de Sauvigny, [3], pp. 82–4.

DOCUMENT 22   THE JULY REVOLUTION (2)

Marshal Marmont, duc de Raguse (1774–1852) was the military commander in Paris during the July revolution.

On the morning of Wedneday 28th crowds gathered and people were very agitated. ... Agitation soon became tumult ... white flags were torn down from town halls and thrown into gutters, people shouted 'Down with the Bourbons!' [The king at St Cloud agreed to declare a state of siege, but Marmont was then left without instructions.] At 3pm the situation was critical. We had prepared for riots, but once the whole population had joined in the revolution, the only possible course of action was to evacuate Paris and negotiate.

Duc de Raguse, [23], vol. VIII, pp. 241–57; also in Bertier de Sauvigny, [3], pp. 86–92.

DOCUMENT 23   THE JULY REVOLUTION (3)

General Chamans was in charge of one of Marmont's columns, and had a sharper perception than his commander of what was happening on the streets.

On the morning of 28th, my aide-de-camp, who had lodgings in the faubourg Poissonnière, informed me that the infantry soldiers nearby were strolling around the streets, drinking and playing billiards with the local bourgeoisie in cafés. [After a day of patrolling the faubourg Saint-Antoine and virtually running out of ammunition, with no prospect of supplies reaching him, he and his column struggled back to base.] The murderous struggle showed no sign of abating and I had lost many brave men, when several infantry officers drew near and told me in a whisper that their men were down to their last rounds of ammunition ... it was obvious that we could not get through to the place de Grève. ... It was already between 5 and 6pm, we had been on the march since 7 am; our men were exhausted with tiredness, hunger and especially thirst, because the heat was intense, aggravated by such a long and relentless conflict.

General Alfred de Saint-Chamans, [25], pp. 491–503; also in Bertier de Sauvigny, [3], pp. 92–101.

DOCUMENT 24   THE PROTEST OF THE DEPUTIES
                29 JULY 1830

The undersigned, regularly elected deputies ... consider it their duty to the king and to France to protest against the measures which the advisers of the crown, misunderstanding the monarch's intentions, have recently forced through to overturn the legitimate electoral system and destroy the freedom of the press.

   Such measures are, in the view of the signatories, completely contrary to the Charter. ... The signatories consider themselves legally elected ... and forcibly prevented from undertaking their duties.

From Guizot, [16], vol. 2, pp. 349–50; reprintd in G. de Bertier de Sauvigny, [3], pp. 129–30.

DOCUMENT 25   BERNARD SARRANS, A JOURNALIST AND
LOYAL FOLLOWER OF LAFAYETTE,
DESCRIBES HIS ROLE

After Wednesday evening, patriots, who saw that the deputies, whom they
had tried to rally, had deserted them, decided, as a private initiative, to proclaim a provisional government composed of Lafayette, Gérard and Choiseul.
... This government, which only existed in the minds of some patriots, had a
beneficial effect on public opinion. [Then there was the meeting of liberal
deputies at Laffitte's house.] [Maguin – deputy for Dijon] said that the deputies should recover the initiative and organise a provisional government.
Crowds were converging on the Hôtel-de-Ville demanding the same. ...
Finally Lafayette arrived and offered to take command of military matters.

B. Sarrans, [26], pp. 234–41; also in Bertier de Sauvigny, [3], pp. 153–7.

DOCUMENT 26   THE LOCAL LIBERAL 'REVOLUTION'

*Charles Weiss, librarian in Besançon and an affiliate of the Bourbon cause, was
appalled by the local liberal 'revolution' and confided his disgust to his diary.*

5 August 1830. An assembly of notables met at 4pm and 100 individuals,
claiming to be the sovereign people, presided over by Guillemet, the former
Imperial government prosecutor and the oldest present, elected by acclama-
tion a committee of 12, to look after public security and take whatever measures were needed. It is disorder and nothing more. All the committee is on the
extreme left and far from keeping the peace, they will cause more unrest. They
decided to send an address of welcome to the new government. Someone suggested they should write it as if to a monarch. Desmesmay, a lawyer, opposed
this fiercely, and carried the day. How far we have travelled in a week!

Journal de Charles Weiss, 5 August 1830, p. 255. The manuscript version of
this diary survives in the municipal library in Besançon. E. Travernier
reprinted extracts in a local periodical, *Les Gaudes*, between 1908 and 1913.

DOCUMENT 27   DECLARATION OF THE CHAMBER OF
DEPUTIES, 7 AUGUST 1830

This declaration replaced the 1814 preamble.

The Chamber of Deputies, taking into account the urgent necessity presented
by the events of 26, 27, 28, and 29 July and subsequent happenings which
resulted from the violation of the Constitutional Charter; Considering in
addition that as a result of this violation and the heroic resistance of the

people of Paris, Charles X, the Dauphin and all members of the elder branch of the royal family are in process of leaving France, – Declare that the throne is vacant in fact and in law, and action is required. Declare secondly that, in accordance with the wishes and interests of the French people, the preamble to the Constitutional Charter is annulled, being offensive to the dignity of the nation, in pretending to 'grant by royal grace and favour' rights that belong to French people ...

The Chamber of Deputies, in accordance with the wishes and needs of the French people, calls Louis-Philippe, duc d'Orléans, lieutenant-general of the realm, and his male descendants to the throne. ... As a consequence Louis-Philippe, duc d'Orléans, lieutenant-general of the realm, will be invited to accept and swear, before the assembled Chambers, ... to observe the modified Constitutional Charter, and to take the title, King of the French People.

Duguit and Monnier, [12], p. 212.

DOCUMENT 28 ROYAL OATHS, 1825 AND 1830

The oath taken by Charles X at his coronation, May 1825

In the presence of God, I promise my people to maintain and honour our holy religion, as befits a very Christian king, the elder son of the Church, and to dispense justice to my subjects; finally, to govern in accordance with the laws of the realm and the Constitutional Charter, which I swear faithfully to observe. May God and his holy apostles come to my aid to observe this oath.

The oath taken by Louis-Philippe, August 1830

I have read the declaration of the Chamber of Deputies and the act of adhesion of the Chamber of Peers with great care. I have weighed and considered all its terms. I accept, without restriction or reservation, all the clauses and promises in this declaration, and the title of *king of the French people* which it confers on me, and I am ready to swear to observe it.

His Royal Highness then stood up, and bare-headed, took the following oath: In the presence of God, I swear to faithfully observe the Constitutional Charter, as modified in the declaration; to govern only by law and in accordance with the laws; to render justice to all in accordance with their rights, and in all respects to act in the interests, happiness and glory of the French people.

In R. Rémond, [161], p. 73.

DOCUMENT 29 CONSTITUTIONAL CHARTER OF 14 AUGUST 1830 – A COMPARISON WITH 1814

No preamble (see above). Articles 1–5 – as in 1814. Old article 6 omitted; subsequent numbers of articles therefore differ by one.

New Article 6. The ministers of the Roman Catholic apostolic religion, professed by the majority of French people, will be paid a salary by the state, along with the ministers of other Christian religions.

Article 7. The French have the right to publish and have printed their opinions, according to the law. Censorship will never be re-introduced.

Articles 8–11 unchanged.

Article 13 – as 1814 article 14 on power of king minus final clause and adding 'without being able ever to suspend or dispense with laws'.

Article 14 – as 1814 article 15.

Article 15. Laws may be proposed by the king, chamber of peers or the chamber of deputies. All laws on taxation must be voted first by the chamber of deputies.

Duguit and Monnier, [12] pp. 213–18.

DOCUMENT 30   THE SOCIAL CONSEQUENCES OF THE JULY
               DAYS

Louis Blanc (1811–82), republican socialist journalist, described the social consequences of the July Days.

The bourgeoisie was triumphant. It had placed a prince on the throne, who owed his authority to its gift alone. The ministers were men whose power and reputation it had created. The modified charter was but a constitution fitted to its used. The legislative power belonged to it by right of occupation, and a moment's confidence in its own strength had been enough to enable it to retain that power in the absence of all constituent authority. ... The bourgeoisie, all powerful in society by its possession of the soil, of capital, and of credit, had now only to provide for the establishment of its political supremacy. The people, on the other hand, too ignorant as yet to desire any share of the civil power, writhed under the yoke of a social system that brought it nothing but oppression.

L. Blanc, [5], vol. 1, pp. 266–7.

DOCUMENT 31   'LA RÉVOLUTION ESCAMOTÉE'

Etienne Cabet (1788–1856), son of a prosperous cooper of Dijon, trained as a lawyer. A republican deputy when he wrote the following criticism of 1830, he later became a prominent socialist.

Who made the revolution? Révolution Escamotée! (A revolution which was smuggled away!)

After the victory, everyone would like to claim to be the victor; often the coward, even the adversary, brag more about their courage and contribution and demand the fruits of victory.

Who were the combatants?

The press, defying the ordinances and threats, gave an example of resistance, and courageously set off the insurrection.

The workers, particularly the print workers; the people, who included in their ranks many old soldiers, and among whom one encountered a hundred times more patriotism and honour than among the aristocracy of birth and wealth; students, especially from the schools of law and medicine and the Polytechnique; young people, especially those employed in commerce; patriots, particularly the *carbonari*, who took up arms spontaneously, without consultation, leaders or direction ...

And the deputies? The famous 221? Not many were in Paris. Among them Audry de Puyraveau, Mauguin, A. Delaborde, Bérard, Laffitte, Lafayette, Daunou, Labbey-Pompierres, Bernard, Bavoux, Chardel, de Schonen, Marschal, Duchaffaut, wanted to put themselves at the head of the insurrection.

Casimir Périer, Sébastiani, the two Dupins, Méchin, Bertin de Vaux, Villemain and Guizot were opposed.

But on the 29th, having fought for three days without the support of the deputies, the people were finally the victors. The Hôtel-de-Ville, the Louvre and the Tuileries were the trophies of their heroic courage. ... Later these same people, instead of benefitting from their generous self-sacrifice, earned only disdain, insults, lies and an atrociously violent response.

What was the cause of the Revolution?

The *juste milieu* claim that the ordinances were the cause, no they merely were the occasion and the signal.

The cause lies in everything that has happened in 40 years: in the love of liberty, equality and independence: in the memory of our glorious revolution of 1789, the wish to revisit the principles of our immortal constitution of 1791; in hatred of despotism, the nobility, the emigration, the *chouannerie*, the Jesuits, the counter-revolution, the restoration and its ruinous budgets, in hatred of the Bourbons and foreign domination. It lies in the sentiments which moved all of France when the Bastille was taken, which made the Empire odious despite its glorious conquests ... in a word ... to rediscover independence and liberty.

E. Cabet, [9], pp. 109–20.

DOCUMENT 32   PÉRIER ON THE JULY REVOLUTION

Casimir Périer (1777–1832) came from a wealthy family with varied business interests. He was involved in insurance, sugar-refining, textiles, iron and coal, as well as being a banker and a regent of the Bank of France. A deputy from 1817, he moved from royalist to moderate liberal in opposition to ultra policies. He was one of the first to oppose the Four Ordinances, but was afraid of revolution and supported Louis-Philippe to bring it to a halt. This was part of his speech to the Chamber of Deputies, 18 March 1831, shortly after his appointment as Chief Minister.

The principle of the July Revolution and consequently of the government which is derived from it is not insurrection. The principle of the July Revolution is resistance to government aggression. France was provoked; France was defied; the country rose to its own defence and it was the law which was triumphant. The principles of the July Revolution and its government are respect for solemn promises and for the law.

From M. J. Mavidal and M. E. Laurent (eds), [19], pp. 682–3.

Documents 33–35 and Document 38 are reprinted in *Les Révolutions du XIXe siècle*, 43 vols, Paris, 1974, vol. 8 (no page numbers, except for individual pamphlets).

DOCUMENT 33   **BUONARROTI'S PUBLICITY LEAFLET FOR HIS BOOK**

Buonarroti, who shared Babeuf's views and was a defendant with him in the Vendôme trial, has published a book ... which will explain the excesses of the Revolution, overcome prejudices, and provide true explanations of what happened. ... The aim of Babeuf's conspiracy was equality ... Buonarroti's book ... rehabilitates the Republic.

P. Buonarroti, [6], p. 4.

DOCUMENT 34   *AMIS DU PEUPLE*: **MANIFESTO 1830**

This was one of the small leaflets sold by hawkers.

Part 3. Aside from general political issues, in which the Amis du Peuple shares the ideas of other patriotic societies, the society has a more special target ... this is the defence of the interests of the inferior classes and the improvement of their physical and moral welfare ... the Amis will show that if the worker is often justified in asking for higher wages, the owner of the workshop is equally often justified in refusing ... because he is often obliged ... to borrow at very high rates of interest ... in order to stay in business.
    The Amis will prove that this problem is caused by the system of credit and the privileges of the Bank. The Society demands the abolition of these privileges.

Amis du Peuple, Manifeste, [1].

DOCUMENT 35   *PETIT CATHÉCHISME RÉPUBLICAIN PAR*
                UN MEMBRE DE LA SOCIÉTÉ DES DROITS
                DE L'HOMME, PARIS 1832

Another republican pamphlet.

Q. What is the Republic?
A. It is a state, whatever its form of government, where law is the expression of the general will. All legitimate governments, in which public interest is predominant, are republican.
Q. What is the general will?
A. It is the will of the majority of citizens.
Q. What is a republican?
A. It is someone who puts public interest before private, seeks equal rights, justice for all, and does all the good for others that he hopes they will do for him.

DOCUMENT 36   **THE RETAKING OF LYON, NOVEMBER 1831**

Count d'Argout, Minister of Commerce and Public Works to Marshal Soult, in charge of the military mission to retake Lyon, November 1831.

Under no circumstances whatever can a tariff be acceded to. The public authorities have no right to regulate the scale of wages; no law sanctions such interference. ... If treaties have been entered into, they can only bind the individuals concerned. The administrative authority, so far from subjecting any one to them, cannot even interfere with the contracting parties. ... Assemblies of employers are prohibited, and can confer no controlling power whatsoever. The meetings of workmen, by which they were preceded, were even more irregular.

Reprinted in Guizot, [16] (English trans) vol. 2, p. 473.

DOCUMENT 37   **VOTES FOR WOMEN**

Jeanne Deroin (1805–94) was a seamstress, who qualified as a teacher by attending evening classes. She was very briefly a saint-simonian, opened a school for poor children in Paris in the 1830s, and was an outspoken feminist, almost alone in 1848 demanding votes for women.

Q. What is woman?
A. No one knows. Some say it is a being which comes from God and returns to him; others deny this.

Q. How does she spend her time?
A. Doing everything and nothing.
Q. What is her status?
A. She has none.
Q. Where does she fit in the natural order of things?
A. Problematical.
Q. Where does she fit in the social order?
A. Even more problematical.
Q. Is she part of humanity?
A. The laws of the land do not include her as a separate entity, nor as a reasonable being. The proposed new Constitution ... denies her the right to vote. Not wishing to emancipate woman as a human being, nor like a cat, dog, tiger, lion, snake ..., it has turned her into a thing which resembles a human being for those who love her, into an animal for those who want to make her servile, into a vegetable for those who believe she has no soul, into mineral for those who break her.

J. Deroin, *L'Opinion des Femmes*, 1849. (This was a newspaper edited by Deroin.)

DOCUMENT 38   **PROCLAMATION OF THE SEASONS,**
                12 MAY 1839

This proclamation was presented as evidence for the prosecution in the subsequent trial before the Chamber of Peers.

The hour of doom has struck for our oppressors. People arise! Your enemies will disappear like dust in a storm. Strike! Exterminate the base henchmen and willing accomplices of our tyrants! Forward! Long live the Republic!

Cour des Pairs, Attentat du 12 mai 1839. Acte d'Accusation, [11], pp. 62–3.

DOCUMENT 39   **LOUIS-NAPOLEON ON NAPOLEON**

Louis-Napoleon was, understandably, an enthusiastic propagandist for his uncle.

The Emperor Napoleon has contributed more than anyone else to hasten the reign of liberty by preserving the moral influence of the Revolution and diminishing the fear which it inspired. Without the Consulate and Empire the revolution would have been nothing more than a great drama leaving behind fine memories but few other traces. ... Napoleon planted in France and introduced everywhere in Europe the principal benefits of the great crisis of 1789, and because, to use his own expressions, *he purified the revolution, established kings and ennobled the people.* ... He purified the revolution by separating the truths which it caused to triumph from the raging passions which obscured them; he established kings by rendering royal power respectable and honorable; he ennobled the people by making them aware of their power and giving them the kind of institutions that dignify man in his own eyes ...

Let us not overlook the fact that everything Napoleon undertook and accomplished in order to effect a general fusion, was done without renouncing the principles of the Revolution. ... To sum up the imperial system, it may be said that its basis is democratic since all power is derived from the people, whilst the organisation is hierarchical ...

Napoleonic Europe once founded, the Emperor would have proceeded in France to the establishment of his institutions of peace. He would have consolidated liberty.

Louis-Napoleon, [18], pp. 34–6.

DOCUMENT 40   MARX EXPLAINS THE RATIONALE OF ORLEANISM

The July Monarchy was nothing other than a joint-stock company for the exploitation of France's national wealth, the dividends of which were divided up among ministers, Chambers, 240,000 voters and their adherents. Louis-Philippe was the director of this company, Robert Macaire [an imaginary swindler, depicted in plays and in the cartoons of Daumier] on the throne. Trade, industry, agriculture, shipping, the interests of the industrial bourgeoisie, were bound to be continually endangered and prejudiced under this system. Cheap government, *gouvernement à bon marché*, was what it had inscribed in the July Days on its banner.

Since the finance aristocracy made the laws, was at the head of the administration of the state, had command of all the organised public authorities, dominated public opinion through the actual state of affairs and through the press, the same prostitution, the same shameless cheating, the same mania to get rich was repeated in every sphere, from the Court to the café Borgne [implying dodgy establishments], to get rich, not by production, but by pocketing the already available wealth of others ...

And the non-ruling factions of the French bourgeoisie cried *corruption!*. The people cried *à bas les grands voleurs! à bas les assassins!*

K. Marx, [20], pp. 48–9. Also in K. Marx, *Surveys from Exile. Political Writings*, vol. 2, ed. D. Fernbach, 1992, pp. 38–9.

DOCUMENT 41   LOUIS BLANC DESCRIBES HOW TO
                ELIMINATE POVERTY

How work can be organised?

The government would be considered as the supreme regulator of production, and invested, for this purpose, with extensive powers ...
    The government would raise a loan, to be used to set up social workshops in major industries. ... All workers who could offer guarantees of their morality would qualify for membership, including the cost of the tools of their trade ... wages would be equal ...
    For the first year, the workshops would be run by the government. Afterwards, things would change. The workers themselves, having more of an interest in the success of the association, [would take over] ...
    In conclusion. A social revolution must be attempted:

1. Because the existing social order is too full of evil, misery, baseness, to survive for long.
2. Because it is in the interests of all, whatever their position, rank or fortune, to work towards the new social order.
3. Finally because it will be both possible and easy to achieve peacefully.

In this new world which we are approaching, one thing more is needed to realise the principle of fraternity. This will be the task of education.

Louis Blanc, *L'Organisation du travail*, edited by J. A. R. Marriot, *The French Revolution of 1848 in its Economic Aspect*, vol. 1, Oxford, 1913, p. 117.

DOCUMENT 42   PROUDHON ON THE ABOLITION OF
                PROPERTY

Pierre-Joseph Proudhon (1809–65), a socialist from a peasant background in the Franche-Comté, was the leading anarchist socialist of his day. He believed that private property should be abolished, or did he?

I have accomplished my task; property is conquered, never again to rise. Wherever this work is read and discussed, there will be deposited the germ of death to property; there, sooner or later, privilege and servitude will disappear, and the despotism of will will give place to the reign of reason. What sophisms, indeed what prejudices (however obstinate) can stand before the simplicity of the following propositions:

1. Individual *possession* is the condition of social life; five thousand years of property demonstrate it. *Property* is the suicide of society. Possession is a

right; property is against right. Suppress property while maintaining possession, and by this simple modification of the principle, you will revolutionise law, government, economy and institutions; you will drive evil from the face of the earth.

2. All having an equal right of occupancy, possession varies with the number of possessors; property cannot establish itself.
3. The effect of labour being the same for all, property is lost in the common prosperity.
4. All human labour being the result of collective force, all property becomes, in consequence, collective and unitary. To speak more exactly, labour destroys property.

P. J. Proudhon, [22], in Kelly and Smith (trans), pp. 214–15.

DOCUMENT 43   A NEWLY ELECTED DEPUTY

Jérome Paturot was an imaginary Orleanist, episodes of whose life were serialised in Le Constitutionnel *in 1843 and later published as a book. Heir to a bonnet-making business, but a man with limitless social pretensions, he has just been elected to parliament.*

In the autumn we arrived in Paris, loaded down with petitions and requests. I had promised my constituency good things from the queen, generosity from the king, gifts from all the ministers. It would take at least the whole session even to make a dent in the promises. My constituents were not kidding; they expected me to deliver.

The session had just opened and with it the impressive world of politics. After the speech from the throne, I made my debut as a speaker when asked to take the oath. I intoned 'I swear' with such conviction that it caused some stir. I noticed a slight smile on the faces of the princes. Being a deputy required a sophistication that was new to me. I had to learn to appear detached, to make grand entrances, to study my best angle, in this I was a total beginner, a mere conscript ...

[To try to deliver the promises which secured his election, Paturot begged an audience with an influential bureaucrat, who brushes him aside with promises as empty as those he gave to his voters.]

We are 200 deputies, busy creaming what can be gained from ministerial office; if anything is going, it's for us and our friends alone. Two hundred of us, that equals at least 5–6,000 clients, powerful men who have organised our elections. Think about it. If the national budget is 1,400 million francs, and the state employs 60,000 officials, each member of the government majority can dispose of 7 million francs and 300 jobs. ... In the past the prefect counted for something, now he is the slave of the local deputy.

L. Reybaud, [24], pp. 327, 330.

DOCUMENT 44   **THE ELECTORATE, 1847**

Duvergier de Hauranne (1798–1881), liberal deputy in the Restoration, ally of Thiers during the July Monarchy, was a moderate Banqueteer in 1847.

According to the latest figures there are 61 colleges which have more than 800 voters, 139 which have between 800 and 500, 87 which have between 500 and 400, 95 which have between 400 and 300 and finally 77 which have fewer than 300. In other words, out of 459 colleges there are 258 with fewer than 500 voters, 172 with fewer than 400, and 77 with between 150 and 300. To take only the last category, there are 77 colleges where elections inevitably depend on a very small number of families, always the same, and the majority of which, in addition to local interests, have personal interests to advance. Put among these families, for a few years, any authority whatsoever which is armed with all the forces of centralisation and can bestow all the favours of administration, and tell me if the temptation will not be irresistible, almost always.

M. P. Duvergier de Hauranne, *De la réforme parlementaire et de la réforme électorale*, Paris, 1847; translated in Collins, [10], pp.110–11.

DOCUMENT 45   **IN SUPPORT OF DEMOCRATIC FRANCHISE AND SOCIAL REFORM**

Alexandre-Auguste Ledru-Rollin (1807–74), son and grandson of scientists, was a notable republican lawyer during the July Monarchy, deputy from 1841 and financial backer of La Réforme. *He wanted a democratic franchise and social reform.*

I say that those who pay the taxes of blood, sweat and silver have the right to participate in the government which disposes of all these riches. (toast) To the improvement in the condition of the working class.

Ledru-Rollin, addressing a Reform Banquet in Lille, 7 November 1847. Cited in Baughman, [41], p. 9.

DOCUMENT 46   **ON THE EVE OF REVOLUTION**

Alexis de Tocqueville (1805–59) was the son of an aristocratic Restoration prefect. He was respected for his study of democracy in America and always prophesied doom for the Guizot government.

It is said that there is no danger because there is no riot, and that because there is no visible disorder on the surface of society, we are far from revolution.

Gentlemen, allow me to say that I think you are mistaken. True, there is no actual disorder, but disorder has penetrated far into men's minds. See what is happening among the working classes who are, I realize, quiet now. It is true that they are not now tormented by what may properly be called political passions to the extent that they once were; but do you not see that their passions have changed from political to social? Do you not see that opinions and ideas are gradually spreading among them that tend not simply to the overthrow of such-and-such laws, such-and-such a minister, or even such-and-such a government, but rather to the overthrow of society, breaking down the bases on which it now rests? Do you not hear what is being said every day among them? Do you not hear them constantly repeating that all the people above them are incapable and unworthy to rule them? That the division of property in the world up to now is unjust? That property rests on bases of inequity? And do you not realize that when such opinions take root and spread, sinking deeply into the masses, they must sooner or later (I do not know when, I do not know how) bring in their train the most terrifying of revolutions?

Gentlemen, my profound conviction is that we are lulling ourselves to sleep over an active volcano.

Alexis de Tocqueville, 27 January 1848, speech to the Chamber of Deputies; quoted in his *Recollections*, [28], pp. 16–17.

DOCUMENT 47   **THE FEBRUARY REVOLUTION**

Flaubert, in Sentimental Education, *described the February revolution through the eyes of his hero.*

The rattle of musket-fire roused him suddenly from his sleep; and despite Rosanette's entreaties, Frédéric insisted on going out to see what was happening. He went down to the Champs-Elysées, where the firing had taken place. On the corner of the rue Saint-Honoré he met some men in smocks who shouted to him:
No, not this way! To the Palais Royal!
Frédéric followed them. The railings of the Church of the Assumption had been torn down. Further on he noticed three paving stones in the middle of the roadway, presumably the beginning of a barricade, and then some broken bottles and coils of wire intended to obstruct the cavalry. Suddenly out of an alley, there rushed a tall, pale young man with black hair hanging down over his shoulders, and wearing a sort of singlet with coloured dots. He was carrying a long infantry musket and running along on tiptoe, looking as tense as a sleepwalker and as lithe as a tiger. Every now and then an explosion could be heard.
The previous evening the sight of a cart containing five of the corpses

collected from the Boulevard des Capucines had altered the mood of the common people; and while the aides-de-camp came and went at the Tuileries, while Monsieur Molé, who was constructing a new cabinet, failed to appear, while Monsieur Thiers tried to form another, and while the King dillied and dallied, giving Bugeaud complete authority, only to prevent him from using it, the insurrection grew in strength, as it were directed by a single hand. Men harangued the mob at streetcorners with frenzied eloquence; others set all the bells ringing in the churches; lead was melted down, cartridges rolled; on the boulevards the trees, the public urinals, benches, railings and gas-lamps were all pulled down or overturned; by the morning Paris was covered with barricades. Resistance did not take long; everywhere the National Guard intervened, so that by eight o'clock, by force or consent, the people had taken possession of five barracks, nearly all the town halls, and the strongest strategic positions. Quietly, and rapidly, the monarchy was disintegrating all by itself. Now the mob was attacking the guardhouse at the Chateau d'Eau, to liberate fifty prisoners who were not there ...

The drums beat the charge. Shrill cries arose and shouts of triumph. The crowd surged backwards and forwards. Frédéric, caught between two dense masses, did not budge; in any case he was fascinated, and enjoying himself tremendously. The wounded falling to the ground, and the dead lying stretched out, did not look as if they were really wounded or dead. He felt as if he were watching a play ...

Frédéric was suddenly shaken by a man who fell groaning against his shoulder, with a bullet in his back. This shot, which for all he knew might have been aimed at him, infuriated him; and he was rushing forward when a National Guard stopped him.

'There's no point in it. The king has just left. Well, if you don't believe me, go and see for yourself'.

G. Flaubert, [13], pp. 285–7.

DOCUMENT 48   DECLARATION OF THE RIGHTS OF MAN
AND OF CITIZEN, 24 JUNE 1793

This declaration was constantly reprinted in full by republicans such as Buonarroti and Blanc.

Article 35. When the government violates the rights of the people, insurrection is the most sacred right and most vital duty of the people.

Duguit and Monnier, [12], p. 69.

DOCUMENT 49   FIVE CONTEMPORARY CARTOONS

*49.1 An anonymous engraving showing Punch (Charles X) attacking Judy
(the Constitutional Charter), July 1830.*

Il y a cent cinquante ans, Musée Carnavalet, Paris, 1980, p. 100.

49.2 'The Besieged'. A family in the worker district of St Antoine use any implements they can lay hands on to drive back the soldiers, 28 July 1830. Lithograph.

Il y a cent cinquante ans, Musée Carnavalet, Paris, 1980, p. 35.

49.3 The Massacre in the Rue Transnonain, 15 April 1834. Daumier's portrayal of the massacre of innocent citizens was probably one of the best-known images produced during the constitutional monarchy.

Lithograph 8, C. F. Ramus, [155], p. 8.

49.4 'The main actor in a tragi-comedy', 29 March 1835. Daumier's cartoon, published as repression and censorship intensified, shows the once benevolent, constitutional, bourgeois monarch thrust his top hat with tricoloured rosette and umbrella aside. His once friendly mask fades to reveal a threatening, assertively regal and militaristic king, brandishing a fleur-de-lis, the symbol of the Bourbons who were deposed in his favour in 1830. He is trampling on the rights of parliament.

Lithograph 11, C. F. Ramus, [155], p. 11.

49.5 'A journey among oppressed peoples, 14 August 1834'. Daumier portrays the vast bulk of Louis-Philippe as a poor imitation of Bonaparte on a white horse, ambling through a desolate landscape scattered with skeletal corpses, oblivious to the problems around him.

Lithograph 7, C. F. Ramus, [155], p. 7.

CHRONOLOGY

1814
April   Napoleon abdicates.
                 FIRST RESTORATION OF BOURBONS.
                 LOUIS XVIII BECOMES KING.
May   Treaty of Paris.
June   Constitutional Charter.
September   Congress of Vienna.

1815
March   EMPIRE. NAPOLEON'S HUNDRED DAY RULE.
June   Battle of Waterloo. Napoleon's second abdication.
                 SECOND RESTORATION OF BOURBONS.
                 The White Terror.
August   *Chambre introuvable* elected.
November   Second Treaty of Paris.

1816
September   Dissolution of the *chambre introuvable*.
                 Legislative elections; economic crisis; conspiracies.

1820
February   Murder of duc de Berri.
June   Law of the double vote instigated.

1821
May   Death of Napoleon.
                 Emergence of the *charbonnerie*.
December   Villèle government formed.

1822
March   Conspiracy of the four sergeants of La Rochelle.

1824

March	Ultra election victory.
September	LOUIS XVIII dies; CHARLES X becomes king.

1825

April	Sacrilege law. Indemnification of the *émigrés*.
May	Coronation of Charles X.

1827

April	National Guard dissolved; economic crisis; *Aide-toi, le ciel t'aidera* founded.
November	Elections.

1828

January	Resignation of Villèle; formation of the Martignac government.

1829

August	Martignac resigns; formation of the ultra government.
November	Polignac becomes Chief Minister.

1830

June	Elections.
25 July	The Four Ordinances.
27–29 July	Three Glorious Days revolution in Paris.
31 July	Duc d'Orléans becomes lieutenant-general. *Amis du Peuple* and the *Société des Droits de l'Homme* are formed.
2 August	Charles X abdicates.
9 August	ORLEANIST MONARCHY. LOUIS-PHILIPPE BECOMES KING OF THE FRENCH PEOPLE.
September	Riots in the provinces.

1831

February	Anti-clerical riots.
March	Casimir Périer becomes Chief Minister.
July	Legislative elections.
November	Revolt in Lyon.

1832

	Cholera
June	Popular unrest at the funeral of Lamarque.

1833   Education law.

1834

February	Law against public hawkers.
April	Law against Associations. Revolt in Lyon.
	Rue Transnonain massacre.
June	Legislative elections – defeat of left.
	Society of the Families established.

1835

May	'Grand Conspiracy' trial.
July	Fieschi bomb plot.
September	Press Laws.

1836

October	Louis-Napoleon in Strasbourg.

1837 Society of the Seasons established.

1839

May	Society of Seasons' rising.
July	Louis-Napoleon, *Les Idées Napoleoniennes*.

1840

January	First Banquet campaign.
May	Napoleon's ashes are taken to Les Invalides.
July	Proudhon's *Qu'est-ce-que la propriété?* is published.
August	Louis-Napoleon arrives at Boulogne.
October	Guizot government formed.

1842

July	Legislative elections.

1845 Economic crisis.

1846

August	Legislative elections.

1847

July	Banquet campaign.

1848

23 February	Revolution in Paris; Guizot resigns.
24 February	Louis-Philippe abdicates.
	SECOND REPUBLIC PROCLAIMED.
	Universal male suffrage decreed.

BIBLIOGRAPHY

PRIMARY SOURCES

For students who can reach the University of London Library, Senate House, Malet Street, London WC1 most of the original printed sources listed below can be read in the Goldsmith's Collection. All are on microfilm too, which makes photocopying sections easy. Only a tiny number of works in French have been included.

1   *Amis du Peuple, Manifeste*, Paris, 1830.
2   Barrot, O., *Mémoires posthumes d'Odilon Barrot*, 4 vols, Paris, 1875.
3   Bertier de Sauvigny, G. de (ed.), *La Révolution de 1830 en France* (documents), Paris, 1970.
4   Blanc, J. J. L. and Blanc, L. *Organisation of Work* (trans), London, 1848.
5   Blanc, L., *History of Ten Years* (trans), 5 vols, London, 1841–44.
6   Buonarroti, P., *Conspiration pour l'égalité dite de Babeuf. Prospectus*, Paris, no date.
7   *Buonarroti's History of Babeuf's Conspiracy for Equality with the author's reflections on the causes and character of the French Revolution* ... trans Bronterre, editor of *The Poor Man's Guardian*, London, 1836.
8   Buret, E., *De la misère des classes laborieuses en Angleterre et en France*, 2 vols, Paris, 1840; trans I. Collins, *Government and Society in France 1814–1848*, London, 1970.
9   Cabet, E., *La Révolution de 1830 et la situation présente*, Paris, 1832.
10 Collins, I. (ed.), *Government and Society in France 1814–48*, London, 1970.
11 *Cour des Pairs, Attentat du 12 mai 1839. Acte d'Accusation*, Paris, 1839.
12 Duguit, L. and Monnier, H., *Les Constitutions et les principales lois politiques de la France depuis 1789*, Paris, 1915.
13 Flaubert, G., *Sentimental Education*, Harmondsworth, 1988.

14   Fourier, C., *Théorie des quatre mouvements*, Besançon, 1808; trans
        G. Stedman Jones and I. Patterson, *The Theory of the Four
        Movements*, Cambridge, 1996.
15   Guépin, A. and Bonamy, C. E., *Nantes au XIXe siècle*, Nantes, 1835.
16   Guizot, F. P. G., *Memoirs to Illustrate the History of my Times* (trans),
        3 vols, London, 1858.
17   Hugo, V., *Les Misérables*, trans Norman Denny, London, 1982.
18   Louis-Napoleon, *Des Idées Napoléoniennes*, 1839; trans B. D. Gooch,
        Napoleonic Ideas, New York, 1967.
19   Mavidal, M. J. and Laurent, M.E. (eds), *Archives parlementaires de
        1787 à 1860*, 2nd Series, Vol. lxviii, Paris, 1888.
20   Marx, K., *The Class Struggles in France 1848 to 1850*, (trans from
        German edition 1895), Moscow, no date.
21   Perdiguier, A., *Mémoires d'un compagnon*, Geneva, 1854–55; trans
        M. Traugott, *The French Worker*, Berkeley, CA, 1993.
22   Proudhon, P. J., *Qu'est-ce que la propriété? ou recherches sur le
        principe du droit et du gouvernement*, Paris, ed. and trans D. R. Kelly
        and B. G. Smith, 1840; *What is Property?*, Cambridge, 1994.
23   Raguse, duc de, *Mémoires du duc de Raguse*, vol. VIII, Paris, 1857.
24   Reybaud, L., *Jérome Paturot. A la recherche d'une position sociale*,
        Paris, 1997; first published anonymously as a serial in the *Constitu-
        tionnel* in 1842.
25   Saint-Chamans, General Alfred de, *Mémoires du général comte de
        Saint-Chamans (1802–1832)*, Paris, 1896.
26   Sarrans, B., *Lafayette pendant la révolution de 1830*, Paris, 1832.
27   Stendhal, *Le Rouge et le Noir*, Paris, 1830; English trans with introduc-
        tion by Margaret R. B. Shaw, *Scarlet and Black*, Harmondsworth,
        1971.
28   Tocqueville, A. de, *Recollections*, trans G. Lawrence, New York, 1971.
29   Traugott, M. (ed. and trans), *The French Worker. Autobiographies
        from the Early Industrial Era*, Berkeley, CA, 1993.
30   Villermé, L. R., *Tableau de l'état physique et moral des ouvriers
        employés dans les manufactures*, 2 vols, Paris, 1840.
31   Voilquin, S., *Mémoires d'une fille du peuple*, Paris, 1866; trans
        M. Traugott, *The French Worker*, Berkeley, CA, 1993, pp. 92–115.

SECONDARY WORKS

32   Agulhon, M., *La république au village: Les Populations du Var de la
        Révolution à la II République*, trans as *The Republic in the Village*,
        Cambridge, 1970.
33   Agulhon, M., *Marianne into Battle: Republican Imagery and
        Symbolism in France, 1789–1880* (trans), Cambridge, 1981.
34   Agulhon, M., *1848 ou l'apprentissage de la république 1848–1852*,
        Paris, 1973; rather misleadingly translated as *The Republican
        Experiment*, Cambridge, 1983.

35   Alexander, R. S., *Bonapartism and the Revolutionary Tradition in France. The Fédérés of 1815*, Cambridge, 1991.

36   Alexander, R. S., 'Restoration Republicanism Reconsidered', *French History*, 8, 1994, pp. 442–69.

37   Aminzade, R., *Class, Politics and Early Industrial Capitalism. A Study in Mid-nineteenth-century Toulouse*, Albany, NY, 1981.

38   Aminzade, R., *Ballots and Barricades: Class Formation and Republican Politics in France 1830–1871*, Princeton, NJ, 1993.

39   Anderson, G. K., 'Old Nobles and *Noblesse d'Empire* (1814–1830); in search of a Conservative Interest in Post-Revolutionary France', *French History*, 8, 1994, pp. 149–66.

40   Atkin, N. and Tallett, F., *The Right in France, 1789–1997*, London, 1997.

41   Baughman, J. J., 'The French Banquet Campaign of 1847–8', *Journal of Modern History*, xxxi, 1, 1959, pp. 1–15.

42   Beck, T. D., *French Legislators 1800–34: A Study in Quantitative History*, Berkeley, CA, 1974.

43   Beecher, J., *Fourier. The Visionary and his World*, Berkeley, CA, 1986; trans Paris, 1994.

44   Berenson, E., *Populist Religion and Leftwing Politics in France 1830–1852*, Princeton, NJ, 1984.

45   Bernstein, S., *Auguste Blanqui and the Art of Insurrection*, London, 1971.

46   Bertier de Sauvigny, G. de, *La Restauration*, Paris, 1955; trans. as *The Bourbon Restoration*.

47   Bertier de Sauvigny, G. de, *Nouvelle histoire de Paris: la Restauration, 1815–1830*, Paris, 1977.

48   Bezucha, R. J., *The Lyon Uprising of 1834. Social and Political Conflict in the Early July Monarchy*, Cambridge, MA, 1974.

49   Bluche, F., *Le Bonapartisme: Aux origines de la droite autoritaire (1800–1850)*, Paris, 1980.

50   Bury, J. P. T. and Tombs, R. P., *Thiers 1797–1877. A Political Life*, London, 1986.

51   Carlisle, R. B., 'Saint-Simonian Radicalism: A Definition and a Direction', *French Historical Studies*, 5, 1968, pp. 430–45.

52   Carlisle, R. B., *The Proffered Crown. Saint-Simonianism and the Doctrine of Hope*, Baltimore, MD and London, 1987.

53   Charle, C., *A Social History of France in the Nineteenth Century*, Oxford, 1994.

54   Charlton, D. G., *Secular Religions in France 1815–70*, Oxford, 1963.

55   Chevalier, L., *Labouring and Dangerous Classes in Paris in the First Half of the Nineteenth Century*, Princeton, NJ, 1981; published in French, Paris, 1958.

56   Chu, P. T.-D. and Weisberg, G. P., *The Popularization of Images. Visual Culture under the July Monarchy*, Princeton, NJ, 1994.

57   Church, C. H., *Europe in 1830*, London, 1983.

58   Cobban, A., *History of Modern France*, 3 vols, London, 1965.
59   Collingham, H. A. C., *The July Monarchy. A Political History of France, 1830–1848*, London, 1988.
60   Copley, A., *Sexual Moralities in France, 1780–1980*, London, 1989.
61   Cox, D. and Nye, J. V., 'Male–Female Wage Discrimination in Nineteenth-century France', *Journal of Economic History*, 49, 1989, pp. 903–20.
62   Cubitt, G., *The Jesuit Myth: Conspiracy Theory and Politics in Nineteenth Century France*, Oxford, 1993.
63   Daumard, A., *La bourgeoisie parisienne 1815–48*, Paris, 1963.
64   Devlin, J., *The Superstitious Mind: French Peasants and the Supernatural in the Nineteenth Century*, New Haven, CT, and London, 1987.
65   Dupâquier, J., and Kessler, D., *La société française au XIXe siècle. Tradition, transition, transformations*, Paris, 1992.
66   Faure, A. and Rancière, J., *La parole ouvrière (1830–1851)*, Paris, 1976.
67   Fitzpatrick, B., *Catholic Royalism in the Department of the Gard, 1814–52*, Cambridge, 1993.
68   Fitzpatrick, M., 'Proudhon and the French Labour Movement', *European History Quarterly*, 15, 1985, pp. 407–30.
69   Ford, C., *Creating the Nation in Provincial France: Religion and Political Identity in Brittany*, Princeton, NJ, 1993.
70   Fox, R., *The Culture of Science in France, 1700–1900*, Aldershot, 1992.
71   Fuchs, R. G., *Abandoned Children: Foundlings and Child Welfare in Nineteenth-century France*, Albany, NY, 1984.
72   Furet, F., *La Révolution de Turgot à Jules Ferry 1770–1880*, Paris, 1988; trans as *Revolutionary France 1770–1880*, Oxford, 1992.
73   Furet, F. and Ozouf, M., *Reading and Writing: Literacy in France from Calvin to Jules Ferry*, Cambridge, 1982.
74   Furet, F., and Ozouf, M., *The Transformation of Political Culture 1789–1848*, vol. 3 of *The French Revolution and the Creation of Modern Political Culture*, Oxford, 1989.
75   Gibson, R., *A Social History of French Catholicism, 1789–1914*, London 1989.
76   Gildea, R., *Education in Provincial France 1800–1914: A Study of Three Departments*, Oxford, 1983.
77   Gildea, R., *The Past in French History*, Oxford, 1994.
78   Girouard, M., *Cities and People: A Social and Architectural History*, New Haven, CT, 1985.
79   Goldstein, L. F., 'Early Feminist Themes in French Utopian Socialism: The Saint-Simonians and Fourier', *Journal of the History of Ideas*, xliii, 1982, pp. 91–108.
80   Goldstein, R. J., 'Censorship of Caricature in France, 1815–1914', *French History*, 3, 1989, pp. 71–107.

81 Gourden, J. M., *Le peuple des ateliers. Les artisans au XIXe siècle*, Paris, 1993.

82 Griffith, P., *Military Thought in the French Army, 1815–1851*, Manchester, 1989.

83 Grogan, S. K., *French Socialism and Sexual Difference. Women and the New Society, 1803–44*, Basingstoke and London, 1992.

84 Guillet, C., *La rumeur du dieu: apparitions, prophètes et miracles sous la Restauration*, Paris, 1994.

85 Hanagan, M. P., *Nascent Proletarians. Class Formation in Post-Revolutionary France*, Oxford, 1989.

86 Harsin, R., *Policing Prostitution in Nineteenth-century Paris*, Princeton, NJ, 1985.

87 Hartmann, M., 'The Sacrilege Law of 1825 in France: A Study in Anti-clericalism and Myth-making', *Journal of Modern History*, 44, 1972, pp. 21–37.

88 Hemmings, F. W. J., *Theatre and State in France 1760–1905*, Cambridge, 1994.

89 Heywood, C., *Childhood in Nineteenth-century France: Work, Health and Education among the 'classes populaires'*, Cambridge, 1988.

90 Heywood, C., 'The Revolutionary Tradition in Troyes, 1789–1848', *Journal of Historical Geography*, 16, 1990, pp. 108–20.

91 Higgs, D. C., *Ultra-royalism in Toulouse from its Origins to the Revolution of 1830*, Baltimore, MD, 1973.

92 Higgs, D. C., *Nobles in Nineteenth Century France. The Practice of Inegalitarianism*, Baltimore, MD, 1987.

93 Higonnet, P.–B. and Higonnet, T., 'Class, Corruption and Politics in the French Chamber of Deputies, 1846–1848', *French Historical Studies*, 5, 1967, pp. 204–224.

94 Hoffman, R. L., *Revolutionary Justice: The Social and Political Theory of P. J. Proudhon*, Chicago, IL, 1972.

95 Holyrood, R., 'The Bourbon Army 1815–30', *Historical Journal*, xiv, 3, 1971, pp. 529–52.

96 Hunt, L. and Sheridan, G., 'Corporatism, Association and the Language of Labor in France 1750–1850', *Journal of Modern History*, 58, 1986, pp. 813–44.

97 Ionescu, G. (ed.), *The Political Thought of Saint-Simon*, Oxford, 1976.

98 Jardin, A. and Tudesq, A. J., *Restoration and Reaction 1815–48*, Cambridge, 1983; originally published as *La France des Notables 1815–48*, 2 vols, Paris, 1973.

99 Johnson, C. H., *Utopian Communism in France. Cabet and the Icarians 1839–51*, Ithaca, NY, 1974.

100 Johnson, C. H., 'Economic Change and Artisan Discontent: The Tailors' History, 1800–48', in Price, R. D. (ed.), *Revolution and Reaction: 1848 and the Second French Republic*, London, 1975, pp. 87–113.

101   Johnson, D. W., *Guizot: Aspects of French History 1787–1874*, London, 1963.
102   Jones, P. M., *Politics and Rural Society. The Southern Massif Central c. 1750–1880*, Cambridge, 1985.
103   Judt, T., *Marxism and the French Left. Studies on Labour and Politics in France 1830–1981*, Oxford, 1986.
104   Katzelson, I. and Zolberg, A., (eds), *Working-class Formation: Nineteenth-century Patterns in Western Europe and the United States*, Princeton, NJ, 1986.
105   Kent, S., *The Election of 1827 in France*, Cambridge, MA, 1975.
106   Kritzman, L. D., *Realms of Memory. The Construction of the French Past*, vol 1, 1997; trans. of P. Nora, *Les lieux de mémoire*, 3 vols, New York, 1996–98.
107   Kselman, T. A., *Miracles and Prophecies in Nineteenth-century France*, New Brunswick, NJ, 1983.
108   Kudlick, C. J., *Cholera in Post-Revolutionary Paris. A Cultural History*, Berkeley, CA, 1996.
109   Lehning, J. R., *Peasants and French: Cultural Contact in Rural France during the Nineteenth Century*, Cambridge, 1995.
110   Le Men, S. (ed.), *Les Français peints par eux-mêmes: panorama social du XIXe siècle*, Les Dossiers du Musée d'Orsay, Paris, 1993.
111   Levêque, P., *Histoire des forces politiques en France, 1789–1880*, Paris, 1992.
112   Loubère, L. A., *Louis Blanc: his Life and his Contribution to the Rise of French Jacobin Socialism*, Evanston, IL, 1961.
113   Lovell, D. W., 'Early French Socialism and Class Struggle', *History of Political Thought*, 9, 1988, pp. 327–48.
114   Lynch, K. A., *Family, Class and Ideology in Early Industrial France*, Madison, WI, 1988.
115   Magraw, R., *France 1814–1914. The Bourgeois Century*, London, 1983.
116   Magraw, R., *A History of the French Working Class*, 2 vols, London, 1991.
117   Mansel, P., *Louis XVIII*, London, 1981.
118   Mansel, P., 'How Forgotten were the Bourbons in France between 1812 and 1814?', *European Studies Review*, 13, 1983, pp. 13–37.
119   Mansel, P., *The Court of France 1789–1830*, Cambridge, 1988.
120   Manuel, F. E., *The New World of Henri Saint-Simon*, Cambridge, MA, 1956.
121   Margadant, T. W., 'Tradition and Modernity in Rural France during the Nineteenth Century', *Journal of Modern History*, lvi, 1984, pp. 667–97.
122   Marrinan, M., *Painting Politics for Louis-Philippe*, New Haven, CT, and London, 1988.
123   Martin-Fugier, A., *La vie élégante où la formation de Tout-Paris, 1815–1848*, Paris, 1990.

124 McPhee, P., 'Electoral and Direct Democracy in France 1789–1851', *European History Quarterly*, 16, 1986, pp. 77–96.

125 McPhee, P., *A Social History of France 1780–1880*, London, 1992.

126 McPhee, P., *The Politics of Rural Life: Political Mobilization in the French Countryside, 1846–1852*, Oxford, 1992.

127 Merriman, J. (ed.), *1830 in France*, New York, 1975.

128 Merriman, J. (ed.), *Consciousness and Class Experience in Nineteenth-century Europe*, New York, 1979.

129 Merriman, J., *The Red City. Limoges and the French Nineteenth Century*, Oxford, 1985.

130 Moon, J. S., 'Feminism and Socialism: The Utopian Synthesis of Flora Tristan', Boxer, M. and Quataert, J. (eds), in *Socialist Women: European Feminism in the Nineteenth and Twentieth Centuries*, New York, 1978, pp. 19–50.

131 Moses, C. G., 'Saint-Simonian Men/Saint-Simonian Women: The Transformation of Feminist Thought in 1830s France', *Journal of Modern History*, 54, 1982, pp. 240–67.

132 Moses, C. G., *French Feminism in the Nineteenth Century*, New York, 1984.

133 Moses, C. G., 'Debating the Present, Writing the Past: "Feminism" in French History and Historiography', *Radical History*, 52, 1992, pp. 79–94.

134 Moss, B. H., *The Origins of the French Labour Movement: The Socialism of Skilled Workers, 1830–1914*, Berkeley, CA, 1976.

135 Moulin, A., *Peasantry and Society in France since 1789* (trans), Cambridge, 1991.

136 Neely, S., *Lafayette and the Liberal Ideal, 1814–1824: Politics and Conspiracy in an Age of Reaction*, Carbondale, IL, 1991.

137 Newman, E. L., 'L'arme du siècle, c'est la plume: The French Worker-poets of the July Monarchy and the Spirit of Revolution and Reform', *Journal of Modern History*, 51, 1979, D1203 microfiche.

138 Newman, E. L., *Historical Dictionary of France from the 1815 Restoration to the Second Empire*, 2 vols, New York, 1987.

139 Noiriel, G., *Workers in French Society in the 19th and 20th Centuries*, (trans), Oxford, 1990.

140 Nora, P., *Les lieux de mémoire*, 7 vols, Paris, 1984–93; also in trans. See [106] above.

141 O'Brien, P., 'L'embastillement de Paris: The Fortification of Paris during the July Monarchy', *French Historical Studies*, 9, 1975, pp. 63–82.

142 Offen, K., 'Liberty, Equality and Justice for Women: The Theory and Practice of Feminism in Nineteenth-century Europe', in Bridenthal, R., Koonz, C. and Stuard, S. (eds), *Becoming Visible: Women in European History* (3rd edn), Boston, MA, 1998, pp. 327–56.

143 Palmer, R. R., *From Jacobin to Liberal. Marc-Antoine Jullien, 1775–1848*, Princeton, NJ, 1993.

144 Perrot, M., 'On the Formation of the French Working Class', in Katznelson, I. and Zolberg, A. (eds), *Working Class Formation: Nineteenth-century Patterns in Western Europe and the United States*, Princeton, NJ, 1986, pp. 71–110.

145 Perrot, M., *A History of Private Life: Vol. 4. From the Fires of Revolution to the Great War* (trans), Cambridge, MA, 1990.

146 Pilbeam, P. M., *The 1830 Revolution in France*, Basingstoke, 1991.

147 Pilbeam, P. M., *Republicanism in Nineteenth-century France, 1814–1871*, Basingstoke, 1995.

148 Pilbeam, P. M., 'A Forgotten Socialist: Ange Guépin', in Crossley, C. and Corrick, M. (eds), *Echoes and Insights: Problems in French History – Essays in Honour of Douglas Johnson*, Basingstoke, forthcoming.

149 Pilbeam, P. M., 'Saint-Simon et Saint-Simonisme: précurseurs du socialisme', in Ramières, A. and Grell, C. (eds), *Le second ordre: l'idéal nobiliaire*, Paris, 1999.

150 Pinkney, D. H., *The French Revolution of 1830*, Princeton, NJ, 1972.

151 Pinkney, D. H., *Decisive Years in France 1840–47*, Princeton, NJ, 1986.

152 Porch, D., *Army and Revolution. France 1815–48*, London, 1974.

153 Price, R. D. (ed.), *Revolution and Reaction. 1848 and the Second French Republic*, London, 1975.

154 Rader, D. L., *The Journalists and the July Revolution in France*, The Hague, 1973.

155 Ramus, C. F., *Daumier. 120 Great Lithographs*, New York, 1979.

156 Rancière, J., *La Nuit des prolétaires, archives du rêve ouvrier*, Paris, 1981.

157 Rancière, J., 'The Myth of the Artisan: Critical Reflections on a Category of Social History', in Kaplan, S. L. and Koepp, C. J. (eds), *Work in France: Representations, Meaning, Organization and Practice*, Ithaca, NY, 1986, pp. 317–34.

158 Rath, R. J., 'The Carbonari: Their Origins, Initiation Rites and Aims', *American Historical Review*, 69, 1963, pp. 353–70.

159 Ravitch, N., *The Catholic Church and the French Nation, 1589–1989*, London, 1989.

160 Reddy, W. M., *The Rise of Market Culture: The Textile Trade and French Society, 1750–1900*, New York, 1984.

161 Rémond, R., *La vie politique en France depuis 1789, vol. 1: 1789–1848*, Paris, 1965.

162 Rémond, R., *The Right-wing in France from 1815 to de Gaulle* (trans), Philadelphia, PA, 1969.

163 Resnick, D., *The White Terror and the Political Reaction after Waterloo*, Cambridge, MA, 1966.

164 Reynolds, S., *Women, State and Revolution: Essays in Power and Gender in Europe since 1789*, Brighton, 1986.

165 Riasanovsky, N. A., *The Teaching of Charles Fourier*, Berkeley, CA, 1969.

166 Richardson, N., *The French Prefectoral Corps 1814–30*, Cambridge, 1966.

167 Roberts, J., *The Counter-Revolution in France 1787–1830*, Basingstoke, 1990.

168 Roberts, J. M., *The Mythology of the Secret Societies*, London, 1972.

169 Rosenvallon, P., *La Monarchie impossible: les chartes de 1814 et de 1830*, Paris, 1994.

170 Sahlins, P., *Forest Rites*, Cambridge, MA, 1994.

171 Savigear, P., 'Carbonarism and the French Army, 1815–24', *History*, 54, 1969, pp. 198–211.

172 Scott, J. W., *Glassworkers of Carmaux: French Craftsmen and political Action in a Nineteenth-century French City*, Cambridge, MA, 1974.

173 Scott, J. W., 'Men and Women in the Parisian Garment Trades: Discussion of Family and Work in the 1830s', in Thane, P., Crossick, G. and Floud, R. (eds), *The Power of the Past: Essays for Eric Hobsbawm*, Cambridge, 1984.

174 Sewell, W., *Work and Revolution in France: The Language of Labour from the Old Regime to 1848*, Cambridge, 1980.

175 Sewell, W., 'Uneven Development: The Autonomy of Politics and the Dockworkers of Nineteenth-century Marseille', *American Historical Review*, 93, 1988, pp. 604–37.

176 Sheridan, Jr., G. J., 'The Political Economy of Artisan Industry: Government and the People in the Silk Trade of Lyon, 1830–1870', *French Historical Studies*, 11, 1979, pp. 215–38.

177 Sheridan, Jr., G. J., *The Social and Economic Foundations of Association among the Silk Weavers of Lyon 1852–1870*, 2 vols, New York, 1981.

178 Shinn, T., 'From "Corps" to "Profession": The Emergence and Definition of Industrial Engineering in Modern France', in Fox R. and Weisz, G. (eds), *The Organisation of Science and Technology in France, 1800–1914*, Cambridge, 1980, pp. 183–209.

179 Shorter, E. and Tilly, C., *Strikes in France 1830–1968*, Cambridge, 1974.

180 Sibalis, M. D., 'The Evolution of the Parisian Labour Movement 1789–1834', in *Proceedings of the 10th Annual Meeting of the Western Society for French History*, Winnipeg, 1982, pp. 345–53.

181 Sibalis, M. D., 'Shoe-makers and Fourierism in Nineteenth-century Paris: The Société Laborieuse des Cordonniers-bottiers', *Histoire sociale*, 20, 1987, pp. 29–48.

182 Sibalis, M. D., 'The Mutual-Aid Societies of Paris, 1789–1848', *French History*, 3, 1989, pp. 1–30.

183 Snyder, D., and Tilly, C., 'Hardship and Collective Violence in France, 1830–1960', *American Sociological Review*, 37, 1972, pp. 520–32.

184   Spitzer, A. B., *The Revolutionary Theories of Louis-Auguste Blanqui*, New York, 1957.
185   Spitzer, A. B., *Old Hatreds and Young Hopes. The French Carbonari against the Bourbon Restoration*, Cambridge, MA, 1971.
186   Spitzer, A. B., *The French Generation of 1820*, Princeton, NJ, 1987.
187   Strumingher, L., *Women and the Making of the Working Class, Lyon, 1830–1870*, St. Albans, VT, 1977.
188   Strumingher, L. S., 'The Artisan Family: Traditions and Transition in Nineteenth-century Lyon', *Journal of Family History*, 2, 1977, pp. 211–22.
189   Tallett, F. and Atkin, N., *Religion, Society and Politics in France since 1789*, London, 1991.
190   Taylor, K., *The Political Ideas of the Utopian Socialists*, London, 1978.
191   Thureau-Dangin, P., *Histoire de la Monarchie de Juillet*, 7 vols, Paris, 1884–92.
192   Tombs, R., *France 1814–1914*, London, 1996.
193   Truant, C. M., 'Solidarity and Symbolism among Journeymen Artisans: The Case of Compagnonnage', *Comparative Studies in Society and History*, 21, 1979, pp. 217–20.
194   Tudesq, A. J., *Les Grands Notables en France 1840–1849. Etude historique d'une psychologie sociale*, 2 vols, Paris, 1964.
195   Vincent, K. S., *Pierre-Joseph Proudhon and the Rise of French Republican Socialism*, Oxford, 1984.
196   Woloch, I., *Transformations of the French Civic Order, 1789–1820s. The New Régime*, New York and London, 1994.
197   Zanten, D. van, *Building Paris. Architectural Institutions and the Transformation of the French Capital 1830–1870*, Cambridge, 1994.

INDEX